CHRONOLOGY AND DOCUMENTARY
HANDBOOK OF THE
STATE OF
ALABAMA

ELLEN LLOYD TROVER,

State Editor

WILLIAM F. SWINDLER,

Series Editor

1972 OCEANA PUBLICATIONS, INC./ Dobbs Ferry, New York

This is Volume 1 in the series CHRONOLOGIES AND DOCUMENTAR
HANDBOOKS OF THE STATES.

Library of Congress Cataloging in Publication Data
Main entry under title:

Chronology and documentary handbook of the State of
    Alabama.

    (Chronologies and documentary handbooks of the states,
v. 1)
    SUMMARY: Includes a chronology of historical events
in Alabama, a directory of prominent citizens, an outline
of the state constitution, and selected documents important
in Alabama's past.
    Bibliography: p.
    1. Alabama--History--Chronology. 2. Alabama--
History--Sources. 1. Alabama--History   I. Trover,
Ellen Lloyd, ed. II. Series.
F326.C55   976.1   72-55
ISBN 0-379-16126-5

Manufactured in the United States of America

CONTENTS

CONTENTS

INTRODUCTION

This projected series of *Chronologies and Documentary Handbooks of the States* will ultimately comprise fifty separate volumes – one for each of the states of the Union. Each volume is intended to provide a concise ready reference of basic data on the state, and to serve as a starting point for more extended study as the individual user may require. Hopefully, it will be a guidebook for a better informed citizenry – students, civic and service organizations, professional and business personnel, and others.

The editorial plan for the *Handbook* series falls into five divisions: (1) a chronology of selected events in the history of the state; (2) a short biographical directory of the principal public officials, e.g., governors, Senators and Representatives; (3) an analytical outline of the state constitution; (4) the text of some representative documents illustrating main currents in the political, economic, social or cultural history of the state; and (5) a selected bibliography for those seeking further or more detailed information. Most of the data found in the present volume, in fact, have been taken from one or another of these references.

The user of these *Handbooks* may ask why the full text of the state constitution, or the text of constitutional documents which affected the history of the state, have not been included. There are several reasons: In the case of the current constitution, the text in almost all cases is readily available from one or more official agencies within the state. In addition, the current constitutions of all fifty states, as well as the federal Constitution, are regularly kept up to date in the definitive collection maintained by the Legislative Drafting Research Fund of Columbia University and published by the publisher of the present series of *Handbooks*. These texts are available in most major libraries under the title, *Constitutions of the United States: National and State*, in two volumes, with a companion volume, the *Index Digest of State Constitutions*.

Finally, the complete collection of documents illustrative of the constitutional development of each state, from colonial or territorial status up to the current constitution as found in the Columbia University collection, is being prepared for publication in a multi-volume series by the present series editor. Whereas the present series of *Handbooks* is intended for a wide range of interested citizens, the series of annotated constitutional materials in the volumes of *Sources and Documents of U.S. Constitutions* is primarily for the specialist in government, history or law. This is not to suggest that the general citizenry may not profit equally from referring to these materials; rather, it points up the separate purpose of the *Handbooks*, which is to guide the user to these and other sources of authoritative information with which he may systematically enrich his knowledge of this state and its place in the American Union.

William F. Swindler
Series Editor

CHRONOLOGY

1528 - 1970

CHRONOLOGY

1528   The first Europeans – the De Narvaez expedition – stopped briefly at Mobile Bay. This was part of systematic Spanish exploration of coastal areas of Gulf of Mexico, begun a decade earlier.

1540   *July 2.* The first land exploration, by armed force under Hernando De Soto, marching north and west from Florida, entered area of present Alabama.

       July 26. De Soto arrived at Coosa, Indian capital near Talladega Creek. After several weeks in area, Spaniards continued westward, taking local chief as hostage and guide.

       October 18. Spaniards defeated Indian forces led by Chief Tuscaloosa, who was slain, in Battle of Mauvilla, fortified Indian town near junction of Alabama and Tombigbe Rivers. De Soto's expedition then continued westward out of Alabama, discovered Mississippi River and eventually disintegrated upon De Soto's death. Three survivors ultimately reached Mexico with their story.

1559   Tristan De Luna led expedition of nearly a thousand prospective settlers from Mexico to Alabama.

1561   De Luna settlement abandoned. Difficulty of supplying colony from Mexico, and disappointment at failure to find gold or other treasure in the area, led authorities to give up the venture.

1629   English colonization southward along Atlantic seaboard led to grant by Charles I to Sir Robert Heath. This first Carolina grant extended "westward to the south seas" and thus encroached upon Spanish claims extending north and west from Florida.

1663   *April 3.* Second Carolina grant, by Charles II to Sir George Carteret and associates, established another claim in conflict with those of Spanish colonial

1663   authorities.

1669   *January 31.* French reconnoitering offered a challenge to both expanding English and long-established Spanish territorial claims. A small fleet under Pierre LeMoyne d'Iberville passed along Gulf Coast and anchored briefly in Mobile Bay.

1699   French expansionists moved in force down Mississippi River; by the Peace of Ryswick two years earlier, France had laid claim to all of Mississippi Valley. Now French expeditions reached mouth of the river and moved eastward along Gulf Coast, discovering Massacre (later Dauphin) Island.

1702   *January 16.* Le Sieur de Bienville founded first French settlement in Alabama, Fort Louis de la Mobile, about 25 miles north of site of present city of Mobile.

1704   Indians, often armed and incited by Spaniards, sporadically attacked French settlement. Ultimately Perdido River came to be recognized as dividing line between Spanish and French claims along coast.

French ship *Le Pelican* landed first group of about two dozen marriageable young women from France, at Mobile. Because of their belongings brought in small boxes (*cassettes*), they became known as the "cassette girls."

1711   Periodic flooding of original site of Fort Louis led to relocation of settlement at present site of Mobile.

1712   *September 14.* Although early French settlements maintained slow growth, French colonizers were impatient for faster returns. Proprietary charter was granted to Antoine Crozat, wealthy Parisian merchant, upon instructions to develop all of Louisiana area (including Alabama).

1714   Second French settlement in Alabama, Fort
            Toulouse, established near present site of Wetumpka,
            as outpost to observe and challenge English
            infiltration of traders and trappers from Carolinas.

1717   *March 19.* Crozat's first three shiploads of settlers
            arrived off Mobile.

            September 6. Heavy costs of colonization compelled
            Crozat to surrender charter to a corporation,
            Compagnie d'Occident, which assumed responsibility
            for developing coastal area. About this time,
            approximately 700 persons were reported in Alabama
            settlements. Following year, corporation leaders
            founded city of New Orleans.

1719   French ship, *Marechal de Villars*, landed first group of
            slaves at Dauphin Island. Importation of this labor
            force was part of plan to develop agricultural
            production in coastal area.

1720   *July 1.* Second ship, the *Hercules*, landed slaves at
            Mobile.

1722   New Orleans became capital of Louisiana,
            culminating nearly a quarter-century of French effort
            to establish permanent and productive colonization
            from Canada to Gulf of Mexico. Mobile, and control
            of Mobile Bay, became key to security of
            southernmost end of this empire.

1732   England renewed its challenge to both Spanish and
            French colonial claims with grant by George I to
            James Oglethorpe to establish new colony of Georgia
            for indigent English emigrants. Like Carolina grants,
            Georgia claims were projected "westward to south
            seas."

1733   Disastrous hurricane destroyed much of Mobile; in
            wake of storm, epidemic broke out.

1735 Fort Tombecbe (Tombigbe) constructed on site of present-day Epes at Jones Bluff, in French attempt to cope with growing English trade competition with Indians. Continued Indian hostility toward French kept French settlements confined to coast and Mississippi River areas.

English challenge became more direct when Governor Oglethorpe constructed first strong point in Alabama at Fort Okfuskee.

1736 *May 20.* English and Indian forces defeated French colonial expedition. This was one of a continuing series of clashes growing out of confrontation of rival claimants in this region. It was also a product of a series of intercolonial wars in which the great European powers probed for opportunities, both in Old World and New, to overcome each other's North American territorial advantages.

1739 *August 1.* Governor Oglethorpe concluded treaty with Creek Indians, defining their borders, making them dominant Indian force in southeastern region and consolidating English influence on Alabama frontier. His Alabama flank secured, Oglethorpe invaded Florida upon England's declaration of war on Spain, further weakening potential Spanish support for France against English colonial challenge.

1762 Final intercolonial war led to major British victories over Spanish forces in Carribean. To compensate Spanish allies for territorial losses in this area, France ceded back territory west of Mississippi.

1763 *February 10.* Treaty of Paris ended Seven Years' (French and Indian) War. France ceded territory east of Mississippi to Great Britain; this marked end of French period in Alabama.

October 20. English forces occupied Mobile. Having

1763   now reached the Gulf coast in their colonial
                expansion begun thirty years before, English
                authorities encouraged steady influx of settlers to
                develop region.

1764   Separate Province of West Florida, covering coastal
                area from Mississippi to Chattahoochee Rivers,
                proclaimed by English agents as further step in
                consolidation of their control of region.

1772   *August 30.* Severe hurricane decimated Mobile.

1778   *March 7.* Abortive attempt to foment uprising against
                British authorities in Mobile. Success of British arms
                in Georgia and other parts of southern colonies
                frustrated most revolutionary efforts in this period.

1780   Britain having declared war on France and Spain, Don
                Bernardo Galvez, Spanish governor of New Orleans,
                siezed Mobile and Pensacola, thus restoring Spanish
                control of all of Gulf Coast from Texas to Florida.

1783   *September 3.* Treaty of Peace signed in Paris; Great
                Britain ceded to United States all claims to territory
                east of Mississippi River, except Spanish Florida. This
                left coastal area of Alabama in dispute between
                United States and Spain.

1786   *January 3.* Undertaking to establish its authority in
                place of former English colonial power, United States
                concluded treaty with Choctaw Indians reserving
                certain lands for tribal use in return for rights of
                citizenship.

1787   *August 18.* Border between Georgia and Alabama
                settled in negotiations between American officials
                and Colonel Alexander McGillivray, quarter-breed
                Indian leader and guerilla fighter.

                South Carolina ceded strip of western lands to United

1787   States, completing northern border of Georgia and adding strip along southern border of Tennessee for future Mississippi Territory.

1795   *January 7.* Yazoo land companies, a group of speculators in promotion of settlements in Mississippi River area, chartered by Georgia legislature. Scandals over involvement of many members of legislature in this project led succeeding legislative session to repudiate the contracts. This cloud upon titles to millions of acres opened for settlement complicated territorial policy for next two decades.

                 October 27. United States concluded treaty with Spain under which Spain purportedly agreed to withdraw from disputed area east of Mississippi River.

1796   United States began survey of southern boundary with Spanish Florida, seeking to establish 31st parallel as east-west border, beyond the border of Georgia which lay a short distance further south. This survey recognized Spanish control of Gulf coastal strip and enhanced importance of Mobile as potential outlet for American trade.

1797   Spanish authorities in New Orleans refused to recognize treaty agreement, pressing claims to area north of 31st parallel on basis of Galvez' conquest of 1780. United States responded by constructing forts on eastern bank of lower Mississippi River, within striking distance of New Orleans.

1798   *May 10.* Congress created Mississippi Territory, including all land from 31st parallel to Tennessee border and from Georgia's western border to Mississippi River. Natchez was named capital for whole territory.

1799   Survey of southern boundary completed. American troops relieved Spanish garrison at Fort St. Stephens,

1799   in first formal withdrawal of Spanish authority from Galvez conquest of 1780.

1800   Territorial census listed 8,500 persons in Mississippi Territory.

First elected legislative assembly, including representatives from Alabama, authorized by Congress.

First county in Alabama, named in honor of George Washington, created by proclamation of territorial governor.

1802   First cotton gin in Alabama erected by Abram Mordecai in present Montgomery County at Coosada Bluff.

April 14. In last of state land cessions affecting this region, Georgia ceded to United States, for $1,250,000, all remaining claims to territory between 31st and 35th parallels. The national government still had to settle claims of the Yazoo companies and their promoters, which were not finally liquidated until 1814.

October 17. Having cleared out the state land claims in territory, United States negotiated first cession of Choctaw lands under 1786 treaty, covering area in southwestern part of present state.

1803   *October 20.* By Louisiana Purchase, ratified on this date, United States opened Mississippi River to domestic commerce, encouraged more rapid settlement in area east of river and increased pressure on Spanish Florida.

November 25. Tombigbe settlement petitioned Congress for separation from "the community on the Mississippi" (Natchez), the first of a series of efforts

1803   to divide up original territory. Alabama settlers
declared that territorial government was too distant
to provide for their needs or interests.

Congressional legislation undertook to settle claims to
lands deeded by Yazoo companies, unrecorded Indian
grants to individual settlers, and grants originally
made by state of Georgia. While this was an effort to
confirm rights of persons already on the land,
"squatters" without prior grantors petitioned
Congress to amend legislation to preserve their
prescriptive rights as well.

1805   United States negotiated with Chickasaws for cession
of another tract of land in southwestern Alabama.

1806   In northwestern Alabama, first cession of Cherokee
lands was made.

Congress authorized construction of roads in
territory, including the Federal Road from Athens,
Georgia to New Orleans. This accelerated flow of
settlers from Georgia and Carolinas.

First educational institution, Jefferson College,
founded in present Autauga County.

1807   Congress amended public domain laws to preserve
prescriptive rights of former "squatters" but
prohibited further entries upon public lands except as
recorded through land offices.

February 19. Aaron Burr arrested in Washington
County on charges of treason against United States.

Town of St. Stephens platted on site of former
Spanish fort.

1808   *December 13.* Madison County, named for Virginia
statesman and now President-elect, created by

1808   proclamation of territorial governor.

1809   *May.* Nearly 300 settlers in territory east of Pearl
                River petitioned Congress to divide Mississippi
                Territory, reiterating complaint that Natchez
                government was too remote to accommodate their
                needs.

                November 4. Sentiment for division of territory
                climaxed in convention of representatives from all
                Alabama settlements renewing petition to Congress to
                act.

                December 12. Territorial legislature created Baldwin
                County, from part of Washington County; named for
                Abraham Baldwin, Georgia lawyer and political
                leader, in accordance with wishes of local settlers
                from Georgia.

                December 26. New memorial to Congress proposed
                creation of a "Territory of Mobile."

1810   Second census of Mississippi Territory showed 40,352
                inhabitants.

                September 26. American frontiersmen, increasingly
                restless at Spanish control of Gulf Coast, captured
                fort at Baton Rouge and proclaimed an independent
                Republic of West Florida.

                October 27. President Madison proclaimed American
                annexation of West Florida from Mississippi to
                Perdido River, condoning frontier action and
                reflecting growing Southern ambition to seize control
                of all of Gulf Coast.

1811   *January 15.* Congress in secret session authorized
                occupation of East Florida if a second foreign power
                (Britain) should threaten to seize it. These
                developments indicated rapidly weakening control of

1811 area by Spain.

First newspaper in Alabama, *Mobile Centinel*, established by Miller and Hood at Fort Stoddert.

1812 *May 14.* Act of Congress confirmed Madison's proclamation of annexation of West Florida and amended legislation on Mississippi Territory to incorporate new area into that territory.

June 18. United States declared war on Great Britain; since Spain was an ally of Great Britain, hostilities could now lawfully be initiated against all Spanish Gulf Coast holdings.

House of Representatives passed enabling act to admit all of Mississippi Territory as single state; bill died in Senate.

Second territorial newspaper, *Madison Gazette*, founded at Huntsville, thus giving media of communication to both southern and northern groups of settlement in Alabama.

December 10. Clarke County created by territorial legislature out of part of Choctaw cession of 1802; named for General John Clarke, Georgia Revolutionary War hero now commanding military forces in southeastern United States.

1813 *February.* Congress passed enabling act directing President as Commander-in-Chief to occupy Mobile, still held by Spanish garrison.

April 15. American troops commanded by General James Wilkinson carried out occupation of Mobile, long coveted by settlers as natural seaway for their produce.

July 27. Indian wars began with Battle of Burnt Corn.

1813   Indians had first been incited by great Shawnee chief Tecumseh to join in league against settlements, then stirred up by Spanish authorities to relieve threat to Florida.

August 1. Mobile County created by proclamation of territorial governor as part of consolidation of seizure of former Spanish holdings on Gulf Coast.

August 30. Indians led by halfbreed William Weatherford attacked Fort Mims and massacred 500 persons among garrison and refugees.

December 23. Militiamen from Tennessee under General Andrew Jackson marched to aid of territory and met growing Indian power in Battle of Holy Ground. Jackson was hampered in these engagements by short term enlistments and conflicting instructions from government.

1814   *March 27.* Overcoming political indecision and shortages of supplies, Jackson attacked major Indian force in Battle of Horseshoe Bend and scored decisive victory which broke power of Indian alliance.

August 9. At Fort Jackson, constructed on site of old French Fort Toulouse, Jackson dictated treaty by which Creek nation ceded lands amounting to nearly half of present state of Alabama.

August 25. With deteriorating Spanish control in Florida, British occupied Pensacola to continue agitation of Indian resistance to Americans.

1815   *February 12.* Outer defenses of Mobile captured by British, threatening to nullify Wilkinson's 1813 occupation. Treaty of Ghent ending War of 1812 relinquished area to United States.

June 29. Monroe County, originally embracing most

1815   of Creek cession of previous year and named for Secretary of State James Monroe, created by proclamation of territorial governor.

1816   House of Representatives again passed enabling act for admission of Mississippi Territory as single state, and again bill died in Senate. This reflected developing strategy of Southern states to create more than one state from slave territory to balance admission of new states in North.

       September 14. Chickasaw Indians relinquished claims to lands south of Tennessee border. Choctaw and Cherokee tribes made further cessions of tracts within territory.

       December 6. Territorial legislature created Montgomery County from part of Monroe County; named for Major Lemuel P. Montgomery, killed in Battle of Horseshoe Bend.

1817   *March 3.* Act creating Alabama Territory passed by Congress, to take effect upon admission of Mississippi to statehood; laws and officers of former territory were to continue in force until new legislature met; St. Stephens designated as temporary capital.

       September 25. President Monroe designated William Wyatt Bibb, of Autauga County, ex-Senator from Georgia, to be governor of new territory. Bibb, who had moved to territory after resigning from Senate, was supported for governor's post by Secretary of War William H. Crawford of Georgia, and came to head the so-called "Georgia party" in territorial politics.

       December 10. Mississippi admitted to Union and separate Alabama Territory came into being.

1818   *January 19.* First legislative assembly in new territory

1818   convened at St. Stephens.

February 6. Legislature created eight new counties: Blount County, named for Tennessee Governor Willie C. Blount, who authorized Andrew Jackson's expedition against Creek Indians; Cotaco County, named for a river and later renamed Morgan County; Franklin County, named for Benjamin Franklin; Lauderdale County, named for Colonel James Lauderdale, an officer under Jackson killed in Creek war; Lawrence County, named for Captain James Lawrence, naval hero of War of 1812; Limestone County, named for a river; Marengo County, named for famous battle in which Napoleon had defeated Austrians (many Napoleonic refugees having migrated to this region of Alabama); Tuscaloosa County, named after Indian chief killed in 1540 battle with De Soto.

February 7. Two more counties were created: Cahaba County, named for a river and later renamed for William Wyatt Bibb, first governor of the state; and Shelby County, named for Governor Isaac Shelby of Kentucky, hero of War of 1812 and aide to General Jackson in drafting treaty of Creek cessions.

February 9. Dallas County established; named for Secretary of Treasury Alexander J. Dallas.

February 13. Conecuh County created from part of Monroe County, name from Indian meaning "land of cane;" Marion County created, named for General Francis Marion, Georgia Revolutionary War hero.

March 9. John Crowell of St. Stephens, government Indian agent, took seat as Alabama territorial delegate to Congress.

November 20. St. Clair County created; named for Revolutionary War General Arthur St. Clair.

1818

November 21. Autauga County created from part of Montgomery County; name taken from Indian village on Autauga Creek.

Second Cherokee cession of land in northwest Alabama.

French Vine and Olive Company founded by Napoleonic refugees at Demopolis in Marengo County, on 92,000 acres of land granted by Congress. Because of inability to adapt to local agricultural conditions, and regular encroachment of "squatters" upon the land grant, project was eventually abandoned and French colony dispersed.

St. Stephens Academy chartered, with public lottery authorized to raise $4,000 to erect buildings.

St. Stephens Steamboat Company chartered, with authorized capitalization of $100,000; first steamboat, the *Alabama*, constructed and launched.

First pig iron made in territory, in Franklin County. All of these economic activities reflected rapid settlement of the region and early eligibility for statehood.

1819

March 2. Congress passed enabling act authorizing people of territory to call constitutional convention as preliminary to statehood.

July 5. Forty-four delegates met in constitutional convention at Huntsville; majority had previous experience in legislation or constitution making in their former home states.

August 2. Draft of constitution completed and signed by all delegates. Mississippi state constitution was primary source of text, with clauses patterned after constitutions of southern states from which settlers

1819

had come. Broadened suffrage, more specific provisions for public education, protection of slaves and popular vote for amending constitution among its distinctive features.

October 25. Territorial legislature convened at Huntsville to complete formalities of petitioning for statehood and to elect two United States Senators to take seats upon admission. A new town, Cahaba, was incorporated as the state capital.

Legislature formally greeted Andrew Jackson on visit from Tennessee, and endorsed his recent campaigns in Florida which, without sanction of national government, harrassed Spanish strongholds and added to pressure on Spain to cede Florida to United States.

November 9. Territorial Governor Bibb chosen to be first governor of new state. Constitution provided for two-year term, with right to seek successive term.

December 1. City of Montgomery incorporated; named for General Richard Montgomery, killed in attack of Continental Army on city of Quebec in 1775. Montgomery's body had been reinterred in New York in 1818, reviving national memories of his career.

December 13. Legislature created seven more counties: Butler County, named for Captain William Butler, popular Indian fighter slain from ambush the previous year; Greene County, named for General Nathaniel Greene, Georgia Revolutionary War hero; Henry County, named for Patrick Henry; Jackson County, named for Andrew Jackson; Jefferson County, named for Thomas Jefferson; Perry County, named for Commodore Oliver H. Perry, hero of Battle of Lake Erie; and Wilcox County, named for Lieutenant Joseph M. Wilcox, killed in Indian fight on Alabama River.

1819

December 14. President Monroe approved joint resolution of Congress admitting Alabama to Union. John Crowell, territorial delegate, took seat as first Alabama member of House of Representatives. John W. Walker of Huntsville took seat as first U.S. Senator. By lot, his term was determined to run to March 3, 1825.

December 17. Mobile granted city charter.

December 22. William R. King of Cahaba arrived in Washington to be seated as second Senator from Alabama. His term was fixed by lot to March 3, 1823. Walker and King represented northern and southern sectors of state: Walker, one of founders of Huntsville in 1809 and president of state constitutional convention, led the "Georgia party" in Alabama; King, a former North Carolina Congressman, had been one of leading "war hawks" in 1812.

Third Cherokee land cession effected in northeastern Alabama.

1820

First federal census listed state population at 127,901 persons.

April 18. University of Alabama formally chartered.

April 24. First United States District Court established in state, with Charles Tait, ex-Senator from Georgia, appointed judge.

May. First session of Alabama Supreme Court convened: Clement C. Clay, future political leader, named chief justice; four associate justices, one for each judicial circuit, were Reuben Saffold, Henry Y. Webb, Richard Ellis, A.S. Lipscomb (who failed to attend).

July 15. Thomas Bibb of Limestone County,

1820   president of state senate and brother of first
              governor, elected to fill out term upon death of his
              brother.

              December 4. Name of Cahaba County changed to
              Bibb County, in memory of late governor.

              December 19. Pickens County created out of part of
              Tuscaloosa County; named for General Andrew
              Pickens, South Carolina Revolutionary War hero and
              veteran negotiator with Indians.

1821   *June 18.* Name of Cotaco County changed to Morgan
              County, in honor of General Daniel Morgan, Virginia
              Revolutionary War hero.

              November 9. Israel Pickens of Greene County elected
              governor. He had been U.S. Senator from North
              Carolina and now was leader of southern Alabama
              political faction.

              December 3. Gabriel Moore, member of both
              territorial and state legislatures, elected to Alabama's
              seat in House of Representatives.

              December 7. Covington County created from part of
              Henry County; named for General Leonard W.
              Covington of Maryland who died of wounds in
              Canadian campaign in War of 1812. Decatur County
              (later abolished) taken from part of Jackson County
              and named for Stephen Decatur, hero of war with
              Barbary pirates who had been slain in duel in 1820.
              Pike County taken from parts of Henry and
              Montgomery Counties and named for General
              Zebulon M. Pike, discoverer of Pike's Peak, who had
              died in Canadian campaign in War of 1812.

1822   *December 12.* William Kelly, Tennessee-born attorney
              in Huntsville, elected to fill out term of Senator
              Walker, who had resigned.

1823   First state bank in Alabama established.
Constitutional convention had written stringent
conditions into bank charters in effort to forestall
speculative investments and irresponsible issuance of
currency which had ruined such banks in other states.
Nevertheless Alabama state bank also ultimately
failed.

December 1. Senator King elected to second term.
Census of 1820 showed Alabama entitled to three
Representatives: Moore (reelected); John McKee, one
of early settlers of Tuscaloosa and veteran negotiator
with Indians; George W. Owen, Claiborne, speaker of
state house of representatives.

December 26. Walker County created in honor of
first U.S. Senator, John W. Walker, who died April
23, 1823.

1824   *December 7.* State ordered survey for possible canal
to be constructed around Muscle Shoals, to facilitate
transportation of goods on Tennessee River.

December 20. Fayette County created from parts of
Marion and Tuscaloosa Counties; named for Marquis
de Lafayette, then making his farewell tour of United
States.

December 22. Dale County created; named for
General Samuel Dale, famed frontier Indian fighter
and scout, later member of state constitutional
convention and first legislature.

1825   Lafayette made triumphal procession through state,
being honored at French colony at Demopolis, at
state capitol and at public reception at Mobile.

Seat of government ordered removed from Huntsville
to Tuscaloosa. Although Cahaba had been specifically
incorporated as new capital city, periodic flooding of

1825   site by Alabama and Cahaba rivers, and sectional rivalries between northern and southern political factions, led to selection of entirely new site.

November 25. John Murphy of Moore County became governor. A former political leader in South Carolina, he had been member of state constitutional convention and elected to state senate in 1822.

December 5. Dr. Henry H. Chambers, military surgeon in Creek Indian War and later influential political leader in Madison County, elected to succeed Senator Kelly, but died en route to Congress following month. Congressmen McKee, Moore and Owen reelected.

1826   *April 10.* Ex-governor Israel Pickens appointed to fill vacancy in Senator Chambers' seat, until election could be held.

December 21. John McKinley, Kentucky-born attorney of Huntsville, elected to fill out Senator Chambers' term.

1827   *October 21.* Disastrous fire swept through major part of Mobile.

Mail service via stagecoach began between Montgomery and New Orleans. Overland travel had developed slowly, after first federal roads of previous decade, since most transportation involved goods freighted by flatboat on many rivers of state.

December 3. Congressmen McKee, Moore and Owen reelected.

1828   Encouraging further development of waterway transportation, Congress granted 400,000 acres along Tennessee River to be sold for financing of Muscle Shoals canal.

1829

January 17. Impeachment trial of three state Supreme Court judges begun before state senate. William Kelley, speaker of state house of representatives, acted as prosecutor; he had also been counsel for debtors seeking unsuccessfully to recover usurious interest paid on speculators' notes. Trial of judges for holding recovery barred by statute of limitations reflected political power of "Popular (debtor) Party." Judges Reuben Saffold, John White and Andrew Crenshaw exonerated by large majority in senate trial.

November 25. Gabriel Moore of Madison County, former member of Congress, elected governor.

December 7. Senator King began third term. Three new members of House of Representatives: Robert E.B. Baylor, Tuscaloosa, veteran of War of 1812 and Creek Indian War, attorney and clergyman; Clement Comer Clay, Huntsville, first chief justice of Alabama; Dixon H. Lewis, Montgomery, member of state house of representatives.

1830

January 16. Tuscumbia Railway Company chartered; first railroad company in Alabama.

Second state census enumerated 309,527 population.

January 20. Lowndes County created; named for South Carolina Congressman William Lowndes, popular political figure and ardent supporter of War of 1812.

September 27. Treaty of Dancing Rabbit Creek extinguished land titles of Choctaws in remainder of Alabama and transferred tribe to Indian territory (present day Oklahoma). First of new series of treaties seeking to clear remaining Indian lands for settlement.

1831

First railroad track – two miles -- laid from Tuscumbia to Tennessee River to link up with water transportation.

March 31. Samuel B. Moore, Jackson County, became governor. Gabriel Moore had resigned to seek legislative support for candidacy for Senate.

November 26. John Gayle, Greene County, speaker of state house of representatives, became governor.

December 5. Ex-Governor Moore elected to succeed Senator McKinley. In House of Representatives, Clay and Lewis were reelected, and Samuel W. Mardis of Montevallo, member of state house of representatives, elected to third seat.

1832

Creeks and Chickasaws ceded remaining lands in Alabama. Although individual Indians had been assured of right to own land after tribal holdings were relinquished, encroachments by land-hungry settlers and "squatters" and ineffective remedial efforts by government agents prompted most Indians to move with tribes to western reservations.

January 20. Second railroad company chartered in state, to construct line from Selma to Decatur, later extended to Tuscumbia.

Legislature reorganized state supreme court, reducing number of judges to three and providing for election by state house of representatives to six-year terms. This was ultimate result of attempted impeachment of judges in 1829 and reflected Jacksonian democratic conviction that judiciary should be subject to popular control.

December 18. Ten more counties created, largely from latest Indian cessions: Barbour County, taken in part from Pike County and named for Governor

1832

James Barbour of Virginia, Secretary of War under President John Quincy Adams; Benton County, named for Missouri Senator Thomas Hart Benton, advocate of western expansion (later renamed for John C. Calhoun); Chambers County, named for Dr. Henry H. Chambers, who died en route to Washington after being named to United States Senate; Coosa County, named for a river and ancient Indian capital; Macon County, named for North Carolina Congressman Nathaniel Macon, states' rights supporter; Randolph County, named for John Randolph, Virginia statesman; Russell County, named for Colonel Gilbert C. Russell, veteran of War of 1812 and prominent Mobile businessman; Sumter County, named for South Carolina General Thomas Sumter, Revolutionary War hero, diplomat and United States Senator; Talladega County, formed from Indian words said to signify "border town;" and Tallapoosa County, named for a river.

1833

First canal in Alabama completed, from Huntsville to Looney's Landing, Tennessee.

November 13. "Stars fell on Alabama" – great meteor shower.

December 2. Alabama's Congressional delegation increased to five; Representatives Clay, Lewis and Mardis reelected; Ex-Senator John McKinley and Ex-Governor John Murphy elected to new seats.

1834

Chickasaw tribe removed to Indian territory.

1835

November 21. Congressman Clement Comer Clay, now one of dominant figures in state politics, elected governor.

December 7. Senator King began fourth term. Congressman Lewis reelected to House seat; new Representatives included Reuben Chapman,

1835   Somerville, member of state senate; Joab Lawler, Mardisville, clergyman and member of state legislature; Francis S. Lyon, Demopolis, president of state senate; Joshua L. Martin, Athens, state solicitor and circuit court judge.

December 29. Treaty of New Echota effected cession of most of remaining Cherokee lands in Alabama. Andrew Jackson, whose victory at Horseshoe Bend had been made possible by Cherokee allies, as President refused to hear Cherokee delegation seeking better treaty terms.

1836   Cherokees began removal to Indian territory.

January 9. Three counties created out of Cherokee cessions: Cherokee County, named for the tribe; DeKalb County, named for Major General Johann DeKalb, Bavarian officer serving in Continental Army who was killed at Battle of Camden, South Carolina in 1780; and Marshall County, named for Chief Justice John Marshall, who had died in 1835.

1837   *January 9.* Legislature abolished all direct taxes, on theory that state bank would finance all expenses of government. Chartering of competing banks in ensuing decade, unsound investments and overissue of bank notes led to collapse of state bank ten years later.

Second Creek "war" broke out, over clashes between land-hungry settlers and individual Indians who had been promised right to remain, after tribal cessions, on "located" tracts of 320 acres each.

April 22. Ex-Senator John McKinley elected to replace Senator Moore; however, before he could take his seat he was nominated to be a Justice of the Supreme Court of the United States and resigned seat without qualifying.

1837

July. Hugh McVay of Lauderdale became governor for remainder of term when Governor Clay was designated to succeed Senator McKinley.

September 4. Clement Comer Clay took seat as U.S. Senator. Congressmen Chapman, Lewis, Lyon and Martin reelected. Congressman Lawler, also reelected, died May 5, 1838.

September 25. John McKinley took seat on Supreme Court of United States.

November 31. Arthur Pendleton Bagby of Monroe was elected to full term as governor. His election represented triumph for Jacksonian party in face of growing Whig strength in state and in hope of extensive reform of state finance, corruption of which had been exposed by nationwide Panic of 1837. Bagby had been youngest speaker of state house of representatives in 1822 and was again serving as speaker when he was elected governor.

1838

Final Choctaw cessions in Alabama.

December 3. George W. Crabb of Tuscaloosa, member of state senate, succeeded to Congressman Lawler's seat.

1839

February 1. Imprisonment for debt abolished by state legislature.

December 2. Congressmen Chapman, Crabb and Lewis reelected; new Alabama Representatives included James Dellet, first speaker of state house of representatives in 1819, and David Hubbard of Courtland, who ran as a "States' Rights Democrat."

1840

Census listed population at 590,756.

Yellow fever epidemic in Mobile caused 686 deaths.

1841   *May 31.* Senator King began fourth term. Congressmen Chapman and Lewis were reelected; new Congressmen included George S. Houston of Athens, William W. Payne of Gainesville and Benjamin G. Shields of Demopolis. Shields was only Whig in delegation, indicating momentary decline of that party in state.

November 22. Benjamin Fitzpatrick of Autauga County, planter and "States' Rights" Democrat, elected governor.

December 27. Ex-Governor Bagby seated as U.S. Senator to fill vacancy left by resignation of Senator Clay.

December 29. Coffee County created out of part of Dale County; named for General John Coffee, Jackson's lieutenant in Creek Indian War.

December 31. Legislature enacted law "to secure more speedily the collection of debts against corporations," an attempt to expedite judgments against defaulting railroads by providing garnishment procedure.

1842   Legislature restored general tax, anticipating collapse of state bank as source of public revenues.

1843   *December 4.* Senator Bagby began full term. Alabama now entitled to seven members of House of Representatives; Congressmen Chapman, Houston, Lewis, and Payne reelected; new members included former Congressman Dellet, James E. Belsen of Montgomery and Felix G. McConnell of Talladega. Democrats claimed all seats in this session.

1844   *May 7.* Congressman Lewis appointed (and subsequently elected) to fill seat of Senator King, who had been appointed U.S. minister to France.

1844   *December 2.* Lewis' seat of House of Representatives
                filled by William L. Yancey of Wetumpka, militant
                states' rights leader and later architect of secession.

1845   *December 1.* Congressmen Chapman, Houston,
                McConnell, Payne and Yancey reelected; new
                Representatives included Edmund S. Dargan, Mobile,
                and Henry W. Hilliard, Montgomery. Dargan was
                mayor of Mobile at time of election; Hilliard was first
                Whig to run successfully for Congress in several
                elections, indicating brief resurgence of party.

                December 10. Joshua Lanier Martin of Tuscaloosa
                became governor. Martin had served two terms in
                Congress and had retired to private law practice until
                drafted by Democrats to run for governor.

1846   *January 28.* Legislature selected Montgomery as site
                of state capitol, following amendment of state
                constitution removing section specifying Tuscaloosa
                as site. The maneuvering to get amendment before
                people, and to effect change in site, reflected
                emergence of "black belt" southern faction as
                dominant political force in state. Montgomery
                businessmen provided private funds to build new
                state house.

                February 4. State bank began liquidation of its assets.
                Unrestricted chartering of other banks, failure to
                supervise investment policies and excessive issuance
                of bank notes had foredoomed enterprise.

1846   *December 7.* Two vacancies in state Congressional
                delegation created by death of Congressman
                McConnell and resignation of Congressman Yancey.
                Two members of state house of representatives were
                elected to fill seats: Franklin W. Bowdon, Talladega,
                and James L.F. Cottrell, Hayneville.

1847   *December 4.* Medical Association of Alabama formed

1847   at Mobile.

December 6. First session of legislature to convene in new capital at Montgomery was also first to meet under amended constitutional plan of biennial sessions.

December 6. Senator Lewis reelected. Congressmen Bowdon, Hilliard and Houston reelected; new Congressmen: William R.W. Cobb, merchant and planter of Bellefontaine; ex-Governor John Gayle of Mobile; Sampson W. Harris, state senator from Wetumpka; Samuel W. Inge, member of state house of representatives from Livingston.

December 16. Reuben Chapman, former Congressman from Madison County, elected governor.

December 29. Choctaw County formed from parts of Washington and Sumter Counties; named for Indian tribe.

1848   *March 3.* Washington & New Orleans Telegraph Company, first such service in Alabama, granted legislative charter.

July 13. Ex-Senator King appointed to fill seat of Senator Bagby, who had resigned June 16 to become American minister to Russia.

December 11. Ex-Governor Benjamin Fitzpatrick elected to seat of Senator Lewis, who had died October 25.

1849   Legislature enacted statute providing for popular election of all judges, an action hailed as democratizing of judiciary.

December 6. Jeremiah Clemens of Huntsville, veteran

1849 of Mexican War and popular political leader, elected to serve remainder of Senator Lewis' term. Congressmen Bowdon, Cobb, Hilliard, Harris and Inge reelected; new Congressmen: William J. Alston, jurist and Whig party leader of Linden, and ex-Congressman David Hubbard, "States' Rights" Democrat of Kinlock.

December 14. New state capitol burned, although most important public records were saved.

December 17. Henry Watkins Collier of Tuscaloosa elected governor. For twelve years chief justice of Alabama, Collier like his predecessor Reuben Chapman represented the moderate element in the state Democratic party holding the balance of power for the moment against the Yancey-led extremists and the remnants of the Whig party.

1850 Decennial census for Alabama showed 771,623 population.

February 4. Legislature voted public funds to subsidize construction of railroad from Tennessee River to Mobile Bay.

February 12. Hancock County created from part of Walker County; named for John Hancock, signer of Declaration of Independence; later renamed Winston County.

July 10. Senator King elected president *pro tempore* of Senate.

September 20. Congress voted first major allocation of public lands for subsidizing of railroad construction; Alabama Congressional delegation, including Senator King who now had become major political figure in Democratic party, succeeded in including rider specifying part of allocation to

1850   Alabama.

October 22. Compromise of 1850, suggesting territorial division between slave and free states, created great political turmoil in Alabama. Group of planters and lawyers -- the "Eufala Regency" – drew up petition requesting special session of legislature to consider secession.

1851   New capitol in Montgomery completed.

Albert J. Pickett published his two-volume *History of Alabama*.

Legislature reduced state supreme court to five justices.

January 9. Union Party organized at meeting in Montgomery, advocating support of Compromise of 1850 and rejecting proposals for secession. Ex-Congressman Hilliard was one of leaders in this movement, which attracted large group of former Whigs.

February 10. Southern Rights Party, long a faction within Democratic Party, formally organized at meeting in Montgomery. Dominated by ex-Congressman Yancey and a number of former South Carolinians, including ex-Senator Bagby and John J. Seibels, Montgomery editor.

December 1. Congressional delegation elected in aftermath of Compromise reflected political schisms: Reelected Congressmen Cobb, Harris and Houston were only regular Democrats in delegation. New Congressmen included James Abercrombie of Girard and Alexander Smith of Talladega, both Whigs, and William R. Smith of Fayette, elected on a combination of Whig and Union party votes; and Judge John Bragg of Mobile, a "States' Rights"

1851   Democrat.

1852   *March 4.* Southern Rights party convention in
                Montgomery failed to marshal sufficient support to
                challenge Democratic organization. With practical
                alternative of rejoining dominant party to work
                toward gaining control of it, trend toward a long-term
                one-party regime in state was already manifest.

1853   Second yellow fever epidemic in Mobile caused 764
                deaths.

                January 20. Senator King having been elected
                Vice-President of United States on ticket with
                Franklin Pierce, he had resigned his seat December
                20, 1852. Ex-Senator Fitzpatrick was appointed, and
                subsequently elected, to fill the seat.

                March 4. William R. King sworn in as Vice-President.
                In rapidly failing health, King had gone to Cuba
                seeking recovery, and was permitted to take oath of
                office there by special act of Congress. He died April
                18, 1853.

                March 25. John A. Campbell, brilliant young
                Alabama attorney, appointed to Supreme Court of
                United States on personel recommendation of Chief
                Justice Roger B. Taney. Although his outspoken
                support of states' rights caused some Northern
                grumbling, Senate unanimously confirmed him.

                December 5. Congressmen Abercrombie, Cobb,
                Harris, Houston and Smith reelected. New
                Congressmen: James F. Dowdell, planter and
                businessman, of Chambers, a "States' Rights"
                Democrat; and Philip Phillips, Mobile attorney and
                regular Democrat.

                December 14. Clement C. Clay, Jr. took seat as
                successor to Senator Clemens; son of Clement Comer

1853   Clay, longtime power in state politics. Young Clay was a strong states' rights advocate and his election followed a stalemate in the Alabama legislature which had left the Senate seat vacant from March 4 to November 28, 1853.

    December 30. John Anthony Winston, Sumter County, became governor. A wealthy planter and cotton broker, and the first governor to have been born in Alabama, Winston at this time was an ally of William Yancey and a member of the "States' Rights" faction of the party. Ascendancy of Winston, the younger Clay and Campbell in state and national affairs indicated the sectionalists had succeeded in capturing control of state Democratic party.

1854   South & North Railroad Co., later Louisville & Nashville, was chartered.

1855   *June 12.* American (Know Nothing) Party organized at Montgomery. A nativistic, anti-Catholic movement which had caught a national interest in secret societies, the party in Alabama and elsewhere found a vacuum in politics left by the disintegration of the Whigs. State party attracted large following – some for its ritual, some for its doctrine but most for the chance to revive an opposition political organization. Aroused Democratic forces waged strong campaign in this year's elections and smashed the threat.

    December 3. Senator Fitzpatrick elected to full term in another triumph of "States' Rights" faction in legislature. Congressmen Cobb, Dowdell, Harris, Houston and Smith reelected; new Congressmen were Eli S. Shorter of Eufala, Democrat, and Percy Walker of Mobile, son of first Alabama Senator John Walker. This association and concentrated American Party votes won him election.

1856   Alabama Educational Association founded.

1857   *December 1.* Andrew Barry Moore of Perry County,
                elected governor; he was last *ante bellum* executive in
                state. Speaker of state house of representatives for six
                years, circuit judge for five, he was vigorous
                supporter of "States' Rights" faction.

                December 7. Congressmen Cobb, Dowdell, Houston
                and Smith reelected; new Congressmen included
                Jabez L.M. Curry of Talladega and Sydenham Smith
                of Greensboro, both Mexican War veterans, and
                James A. Stallworth, Evergreen attorney. All were
                Democrats, formally or informally committed to the
                "States' Rights" faction.

1858   *January 22.* Hancock County renamed Winston
                County, in honor of former governor and first native
                Alabamian in that office.

                January 29. Benton County renamed Calhoun
                County in honor of South Carolina statesman. Both
                actions of renaming counties reflected mounting
                sectionalist excitement in state.

                August 1. Alabama Institute for Deaf, Dumb and
                Blind opened in Talladega.

1859   Medical College of Alabama, affiliated with state
                university, opened in Mobile.

                William L. Yancey proposed organization of a League
                of United Southerners from various slave states to
                seize control of national Democratic Party before
                conventions of 1860.

                December 5. Congressmen Cobb, Curry, Houston,
                Moore and Stallworth reelected; new Congressmen
                included David Clopton, Tuskegee attorney, and
                James L. Pugh, farmer of Eufala.

1860   Decennial census listed 964,201 population.

1860

January 11. Democratic state convention split over question of Presidential candidates to be voted on at national convention. Yancey faction dominated state group but separate factions organized to pledge support to compromise candidates.

February. Legislature instructed Governor Moore to plan to call convention in event of election of "a President advocating the principles and action of the party in the Northern States calling itself the Republican Party."

June 27. Constitutional Union Party organized in state to support candidacy of John Bell of Tennessee and Edward Everett of Massachusetts. Party, in Alabama and nationally, consisted of remnants of Whig and American Parties and opposed sectionalist programs of other parties.

June 28. Yancey faction of state Democratic party joined with other Southern states in convention at Baltimore to nominate John C. Breckenridge of Kentucky and Joseph Lane of Oregon.

November 6. In Presidential election, Alabama voted for the Breckenridge-Lane ticket of the secessionist faction.

December 6. Governor Moore called for a special election for delegates to a convention of the people of Alabama, as provided by legislative resolution of preceding February.

December 24. General election of convention delegates held. Of 100 selected, 54 were advocates of immediate secession and 46 advocated "cooperation" with other Southern states in appropriate joint action. South Carolina had seceded December 20.

1861

January 4. Alabama troops seized federal arsenal at

1861   Mt. Vernon.

January 5. Alabama troops occupied Forts Gaines and Morgan, commanding approaches to Mobile Bay. On this date, President Buchanan ordered a supply ship to attempt to reach Fort Sumter in harbor of Charleston, S.C.

January 7. Convention opened in Montgomery. Secessionist majority elected William McLin Brooks of Perry County as president of convention, but William L. Yancey was majority leader. Ex-Senator Clemens was one of leaders of "cooperation" faction.

January 11. Ordinance of Secession, largely drafted by Yancey, adopted by convention, 61-39. In addition to declaring that Alabama "is, and of right ought to be, a Sovereign and Independent State," ordinance called upon other Southern states to meet February 4 to determine upon joint action.

First state flag of Alabama formally presented to convention, to take place of Stars and Stripes. Original flag captured by Iowa troops in course of Civil War and formally returned by state of Iowa in 1938.

January 21. Entire Alabama delegation in Congress formally resigned their seats. All had been reelected in November 1860.

February 4. Provisional Congress of Confederate States convened at Montgomery, pursuant to invitation of Alabama convention. The Alabama delegation was predominantly moderates, and Yancey had been excluded as concession to moderate sentiment. Delegates included William P. Chilton, state supreme court justice, ex-Congressman Jabez L.M. Curry, Dr. Thomas Fearn, Colin J. McRae, and R.W. Walker, both planters. Of these, only Curry was

1861   radical secessionist.

February 8. Constitution for the Confederate States of America adopted by provisional congress; text closely resembled federal Constitution, which Yancey and others declared would have been acceptable had it not been violated by Northern abolitionists. New Constitution specifically forbade importation of slaves from abroad, a bid for British and French support.

February 9. Jefferson Davis of Mississippi and Alexander H. Stephens of Georgia elected President and Vice-President of Confederate States of America. Provisional congress was declared to continue until elections could be held in November.

Alabama legislature lent $500,000 to new Confederate government until a new revenue system could be established within Confederate States.

May 21. Confederate Congress voted to move capital from Montgomery to Richmond, Va.

LeRoy Pope Walker, son of the first U.S. Senator from Alabama, was named first Secretary of War in President Davis' cabinet.

November. William L. Yancey and Clement C. Clay, Jr. named first Confederate Senators from Alabama. State delegation to Confederate Congress, first session, included ex-U.S. Congressmen Edmund J. Dargan, Jabez L.M.Curry, Francis Lyon, James L. Pugh and William R. Smith.

December 2. John Gill Shorter inaugurated first governor of Alabama under Confederacy. Brother of ex-Congressman Eli Sims Shorter, an enthusiastic secessionist and member of provisional Confederate Congress, his election was hailed as evidence of state

1861   support of Davis administration.

1862   *March*. Thomas Hill Watts of Montgomery appointed
                attorney general of Confederate States.

                April 8. Huntsville occupied by Union troops. From
                several adjacent bases in northern Alabama, Union
                raiders began series of harassments of towns and
                communications throughout Tennessee Valley.

1863   *August*. Legislature enacted series of emergency
                statutes to meet worsening military situation:
                $1,000,000 appropriated for support of service
                families for year; conscription for armed forces
                decreed for all males between 16 and 60 years of age.

                November. Legislature appropriated additional
                $1,500,000 for state defenses, and levied 10 percent
                tax on all products.

                December 1. Thomas Hill Watts elected governor.
                Originally a secessionist, his service in Davis' cabinet
                had disillusioned him with Confederacy and his brief
                administration was divided between seeking to resist
                Union military invasion of State and Confederate
                demands for conscription of materials.

                Second Confederate Congress also reflected Alabama
                disaffection with Davis administration. R.W. Walker
                defeated Senator Clay in Clay's bid for second term,
                and Robert W. Jemison, oldline Whig, was named to
                seat vacated by death of Senator Yancey.

                December 16. Union troops invested Pensacola,
                preparing way for harassment of Confederate
                defenses along Gulf Coast.

1864   *August 5*. Admiral David Farragut ("damn the
                torpedoes") defeated Confederate land and sea forces
                in Battle of Mobile Bay.

1864   *August 6*. Union troops captured Fort Gaines.

                August 23. Union troops captured companion Fort
                Morgan, thus opening way for land invasion and
                ultimate attack on Mobile.

                December 15. Large Union forces invaded Alabama
                from Tennessee and Georgia, driving to link up with
                armies landing on Gulf Coast following Farragut's
                naval triumph.

1865   *April 1*. Confederate forces in Selma destroyed
                20,000 bales of cotton before retreating from city,
                which fell to Union troops on following day.

                April 4. Union troops destroyed large part of campus
                of University of Alabama.

                April 12. Both cities of Mobile and Montgomery
                surrendered to Union armies as Confederate
                resistance disintegrated. On this same day, William
                Crawford Bibb as official agent of Governor Watts
                met with President Lincoln in Washington to discuss
                means of continuing civil government in Alabama.

                May 4. General Richard Taylor surrendered remnants
                of Confederate forces in Department of the West at
                Citronelle. Martial law was proclaimed and civil
                government ceased to operate until provisional
                government was established June 21.

                June 21. Lewis E. Parsons of Talladega, a pre-war
                Douglas Democrat, named provisional governor of
                Alabama by President Andrew Johnson, with
                instructions to reestablish offices of civil government
                and prepare for new state constitutional convention.

                July 20. Governor Parsons issued call for election for
                delegates to new constitutional convention. In
                separate proclamations he announced conditions

1865

under which citizenship could be restored with right to vote. Since conditions required taking amnesty oath and this was limited to persons not "leaders of rebellion" or owners of more than $20,000 property value, majority of experienced political figures were disfranchised.

August 31. In vote for constitutional convention delegates, fewer than 30,000 out of 56,825 registered persons cast ballots.

September 12. Constitutional convention met in Montgomery. Of 100 delegates, 99 attended; they included ex-Senator and ex-Governor Benjamin Fitzpatrick, ex-Congressman Alexander White and ex-Governor John W. Winston. Fitzpatrick was elected president of convention.

September 30. New state constitution adopted and convention adjourned. Among other things, convention had declared null and void 1861 ordinance of secession and all other ordinances in conflict with federal Constitution; adopted 13th Amendment and reiterated abolition of slavery in state constitution; repudiated war debt; and provided for election of new officers of civil government.

November 6. First election under new constitution resulted in victory of Robert M. Patton of Lauderdale County, oldtime Whig and president of state senate in 1861, as governor. Patton was inaugurated December 13 but it was not until December 20 that Governor Parsons received instructions from Secretary of State William H. Seward to turn over the office.

November 28. Legislature elected new U.S. Senators: ex-Governor Parsons for full term and ex-Congressman George S. Houston for short term. Congress refused to seat them, as well as six elected Congressmen: Cullen A. Battle of Tuskegee, Thomas

1865   J. Foster of Lawrence County, George C. Freeman of Lowndes County, Charles Langdon of Mobile, Burwell D. Pope of Gadsden and Joseph W. Taylor of Tuscaloosa. Radical reconstructionists had gained control of Congress and rejected Presidential plan of restoration of normal state government and representation.

To resume fiscal operations, state treasury negotiated loan of $35,000.

1866   *January 16.* Legislature memorialized President Johnson to withdraw federal troops from state.

February 15. Elmore County created from part of Autauga County; named for General John A. Elmore, Revolutionary War hero of South Carolina and early Alabama planter.

February 22. Legislature in resolution endorsed President Johnson's reconstruction policy and denounced all persons within state who were falsely representing conditions to national government.

April 2. President Johnson proclaimed official end to state of insurrection in Alabama and other seceded states. Congressional reconstruction plans nullified Johnson's policy.

June. Governor Patton traveled to St. Louis in effort to purchase supplies of corn to relieve widespread shortages in Alabama caused by destruction of plantation economy.

August 2. State convention at Selma elected delegates to national convention of Conservative Union Party in Philadelphia, made up of oldtime Democrats supporting Presidential reconstruction.

November 24. Crenshaw County created from part of

1866   Butler County; named for Judge Anderson Crenshaw, early settler and political leader.

December 5. Lee County created from part of Russell County; named for General Robert E. Lee.

December 6. Legislature on advice of Governor Patton refused to ratify 14th Amendment to Constitution. On same day it created Cleburne County from parts of Cherokee and Calhoun Counties; named for General Patrick R. Cleburne, Arkansas military hero known as the "Stonewall of the West," who was killed in battle in 1864.

December 7. Two more counties created: Baine County, carved from six neighboring counties and named for Colonel D.W. Baine of Lowndes County (later renamed Etowah County); and Clay County, named for Senator Henry Clay of Kentucky.

December 8. Bullock County created from Barbour, Macon, Montgomery and Pike counties; named for Col. Edward C. Bullock, early political leader and one of first state casualties in war. Many new counties created at this time for several reasons: to increase local representation in state legislature; to reduce size of areas for which county governments had to provide public services and raise taxes; and to honor number of recent public heroes of war.

"Patton money," term applied to $400,000 in state certificates issued to meet fiscal emergency in state.

President of University of Alabama traveled to New York to sell $70,000 worth of state bonds for reconstruction of university.

1867   *January 30.* Hale County created, out of part of Greene County; named for Stephen Fowler Hale, Alabama member of Provisional Confederate

1867   Congress and later Confederate army officer killed in
              1862.

              February 4. Jones County created out of part of
              Fayette County and named for E.P. Jones of Fayette
              (later renamed Sanford County and still later
              renamed Lamar County).

              February 6. Colbert County created from part of
              Lauderdale County; named for George and Levi
              Colbert, educated Chickasaw Indian brothers who
              had negotiated land cessions to United States.

              February 19. Legislature passed act "to establish a
              system of internal improvements" by pledging state
              credit toward construction of new railroad and other
              services.

              March 2. Radical Congress passed first
              Reconstruction Act placing southern states under
              military control. Alabama, Florida and Georgia were
              in Military District No. 3.

              March 23. Second Reconstruction Act prescribed
              manner of framing new state constitutions and
              ratifying 14th Amendment as condition of
              readmission to Union.

              April 1. General John Pope arrived in Montgomery to
              set up military government for Third District.

              May 1. General Wager Swayne, commander of
              Alabama sub-district, called convention of freedmen
              to organize political program.

              June 4. Union Republican Party convention held in
              Mobile.

              August. Registration of new voters under
              Reconstruction Acts completed, preparatory to call

1867 for new constitutional convention.

September 14. Conservative Union party convention held in Mobile.

October 1. Election to determine whether constitutional convention should be held and to elect delegates; polls were kept open to October 5 to insure largest turnout of vote for Radical candidates. In this period, 71,730 black votes and 18,553 white votes were cast.

November 5. Constitutional convention opened in Montgomery. Of 100 delegates, 96 were identified as Republicans, including 17 blacks and 28 "carpetbaggers." Elisha W. Peck, Tuscaloosa attorney, elected president of convention.

November 22. Ex-Senator John A. Winston elected by legislature to full term succeeding Senator Houston. Like Houston, Winston was refused seat by Senate.

December 6. Constitutional convention adjourned after drafting new constitution according to terms of Reconstruction Act which also required submission to popular vote. In other actions, convention abolished Baine, Colbert and Jones Counties, established by legislature earlier in year.

New constitution had many modernizing features which were retained by later constitutions: equal rights for both sexes and all races, guarantee of public education, development and supervision of industry, abolition of property qualifications for electoral rights.

December 28. General George G. Meade succeeded General Pope in command of Third Military District.

1868   *January 14.* General Julius Hayden replaced General Swayne as commander of Alabama sub-district. On same day, executive committee of Conservative Party issued request to all white citizens to boycott vote on new constitution.

February 4. Voting on new constitution began. Although voting days were extended to February 8, General Meade declared after ballots were counted that total was 15,000 votes short of required majority.

June 12. Congress by resolution confirmed ratification of new constitution, declared William H. Smith elected governor and admitted Alabama Congressional delegation. Radical reconstructionists were now eager to return southern states to union and have benefit of controlled electoral vote in Presidential elections that fall.

July 14. William H. Smith of Randolph County inaugurated as governor, having been "appointed" by General Meade following Congressional action. Smith had been an ardent Unionist in 1861 and later organized troop of Alabama Union cavalry during operations in northern Alabama.

July 21. Five of Alabama's new Representatives admitted to Congress: Charles W. Buckley, Montgomery; Benjamin W. Norris, Elmore; Charles W. Pierce, Elmore; John B. Collis, Huntsville; Dr. Thomas Haughey, Decatur. Four of five were "carpetbaggers" and Republicans.

July 22. Sixth Alabama Congressman, Francis M. Kellogg of Mobile, "carpetbagger" and Republican, was seated.

July 25. Two U.S. Senators selected by "carpetbag" legislature under new constitution were seated.

1868   George E. Spencer of Decatur, elected to short term expiring March 3, 1871; and Willard Warner, Montgomery, elected to full term expiring March 3, 1873. Spencer was New Yorker who had taken up law practice in Alabama after war; Warner was Ohioan who served in Ohio legislature after war before returning to Alabama to become planter. Both men had won field promotions as general officers in Union army.

August 6. Covington County renamed Jones County, for county of that name abolished by constitutional convention; later in session, legislature restored name of Covington.

October 8. Jones County reestablished by legislature.

November 3. Alabama's electoral votes were cast for Ulysses S. Grant and Schuyler Colfax for President and Vice-President.

December 1. Baine County reestablished and renamed Etowah County.

December 10. Escambia County created from part of Conecah County and named for river.

December 22. Geneva County created and named for Geneva, Switzerland.

December 30. Baker County (later renamed Chilton) created from part of Autauga County; named for Albert Baker, leading public figure in Autauga.

1869   *January 1.* Freedman's Bureau terminated by act of Congress. Begun in 1865 as federal agency to aid newly freed slaves, bureau was converted following year into office to investigate and prosecute state officers enforcing "black codes." It had been subject to widespread corruption thereafter.

1869   *April.* Rebuilt University of Alabama opened its
                doors.

                August 3. New Alabama Congressional delegation
                chosen. Congressman Buckley was reelected;
                Congressman Haughey, seeking reelection, had been
                assassinated. New Representatives included Alfred E.
                Buck of Mobile, Peter M. Dox of Huntsville, Charles
                Hays of Eutaw, Robert S. Heflin of Opelika, and
                William C. Sherrod were both Confederate veterans.
                Haughey's murder by a carpetbagger missionary was
                not related to election, which was generally
                interpreted as return toward normal political balance
                in state.

                October 8. Jones County, renamed Safford County
                for H.C. Safford of Cherokee.

                November 16. Legislature ratified 15th Amendment
                to Constitution.

                December 26. Legislature passed legislation to
                suppress activities of Ku Klux Klan.

1870   *February 21.* Railroad construction boom in state
                caused legislature to pass act reviving prewar
                regulations over railroads in effort to protect state
                and local governments from exploitation.

                November 8. Democratic candidates for governor and
                state house of representatives won elections. Robert
                B. Lindsay of Colbert County, by avoiding direct
                attack on carpetbaggers, won narrow victory over
                Governor Smith and after disputed canvass of votes
                was inaugurated November 26. Stalemate between
                two houses of state legislature doomed Lindsay
                administration to ineffective program for dealing with
                railroad inflation.

                First post-war census listed 996,992 population.

1870   *December 7.* Judge George Goldthwaite elected as Democrat to seat of Senator Warner. An early settler in Pike County, Goldthwaite had served on state supreme court before war and although reelected as circuit judge in 1868 had been disqualified for Confederate military service. His selection was regarded less as Democratic resurgence as defeat for Warner at hands of his his colleague, Senator Spencer, who was intent on total control of federal patronage in Alabama.

1871   *January 1.* Alabama & Chattanooga Railroad defaulted on interest on its bonds. Governor Lindsay seized railroad property to protect state interest. This was one of several railroads endorsed by state officials in order to improve its credit in bond market. One of consequences of endorsement was requirement that counties vote subscription of revenues to aid railroad construction in their areas. Widespread corruption resulted from practice.

March 4. Newly elected Alabama Congressional delegation seated. Representatives Buckley, Dox and Hays reelected; new Congressmen included William A. Handley of Roanoke, Joseph H. Sloss of Tuscumbia and Benjamin S. Turner of Selma. Turner was Republican and black, Handley and Sloss were Democrats and Confederate veterans.

September 26. James H. Clanton, oldline Whig and reorganizer of state Democratic party after war, was assassinated at Knoxville, Tennessee.

December 19. City of Birmingham incorporated by legislature; begun previous August by Elyton Land Company, it had grown to population of 12,000 by this date.

1872   *January 15.* Senate concluded eleven months of testimony in contested seat of Senator Goldthwaite,

1872   decided in his favor and seated him.

February 26. Agricultural and Mechanical College (Alabama Polytechnic Institute) chartered by legislature. On this same date, legislature adjourned after stormy session exposing railroad scandals involving Senator Spencer and Governors Lindsay and Smith.

June 19. State Democratic convention met to nominate state candidates. Exposure of corruption in state offered opportunity to wipe out remnants of carpetbag regime, but party's subsequent endorsement of Liberal Republican ticket of Horace Greeley for President was unpopular with state voters.

August 12. Republican state convention faced threat of defeat of its candidates and its boss, Senator Spencer, who needed control of legislature to gain second term. Spencer's candidate for governor, David P. Lewis of Madison County, was nominated.

November 5. Lewis won election for governor but Democrats appeared to have won majority in legislature. Democrats met at statehouse ("capitol assembly") and elected Francis W. Sykes to be U.S. Senator. Republicans contesting election met at Montgomery courthouse ("courthouse assembly") and reelected Senator Spencer. The state's electoral votes were ordered cast for the reelection of President Grant and Vice-President Henry Wilson.

December 5. Governor Lewis summoned federal troops to capital on day selection of U.S. Senator was to be official. Governor alleged that several Democratic legislators were invalidly elected, thus warranting a finding of Spencer's reelection. Commissions sent to President Grant were referred to Attorney General George H. Williams, who proposed

1872   plan for merging two legislatures in state. Under plan
        adapted, majority vote was found for Spencer.

1873   *March 7.* Senate heard evidence contesting Spencer's
        seat but rejected it and seated him for second term.

        April 19. Legislature passed new series of statutes
        regulating railroad rates and requiring "equal
        accommodation" of races on all carriers. Legislature
        then voted largescale issuance of state bonds virtually
        refinancing several millions of dollars in fraudulent
        railroad bonds. This led before end of year to virtual
        bankruptcy of state itself.

        December 1. Alabama entitled to eight
        Representatives in new Congress. Congressmen Hays
        and Sloss reelected; others included Frederick G.
        Bromberg, Democrat-Liberal Republican of Mobile;
        John H. Caldwell, Democrat and Confederate veteran
        of Jacksonville; Charles Pelham, Republican and
        Confederate veteran of Talladega; James T. Rapier,
        Republican Negro from Montgomery; and two
        at-large members, Charles C. Sheats of Decatur and
        ex-Congressman Alexander White of Selma, both
        Republican.

        December 9. State Normal and Industrial School for
        Negroes opened in Huntsville.

        Cholera epidemic swept Birmingham, yellow fever in
        Mobile.

1874   *July 29.* Democratic and Conservative party
        convention in Montgomery, resolved on solidarity to
        end reconstructionist control of state. George Smith
        Houston of Limestone County, veteran member of
        Congress, 1841-49 and 1851-61, nominated for
        governor.

        November 3. Houston led complete Democratic

1874   sweep of state offices for first time in decade. Practical end of carpetbag rule in Alabama.

December 10. First order of business for new legislature was committee to study need for new constitutional convention. Committee report strongly endorsed call for such convention and legislature approved by resolution.

December 17. Baker County renamed Chilton County in honor of ex-Congressman William Parrish Chilton of Montgomery, former chief justice of state and member of Confederate Congress.

1875   *August 3.* After vigorous campaign for and against proposal for constitutional convention, proposal carried by vote of 77,763 to 59,928. Resurgent ante bellum planter class advocating new constitution was given epithet of "bourbon," which was accepted thereafter as title of distinction.

September 8. Constitutional convention opened. LeRoy Pope Walker, son of first U.S. Senator from Alabama and himself first Secretary of War under Confederacy, elected president of convention.

October 5. Convention completed new constitution, preparatory to submitting it to people. It abolished disability provisions of reconstruction constitution and provisions for state aid to railroads, reorganized public education on segregated basis, retained provisions for manhood suffrage and women's rights.

November 16. Vote for new constitution: 85,662 for, 29,217 against.

December 6. New session of Congress, with Representatives elected previous year, reflected completeness of Democratic return to power. Only Republican reelected was Congressman Hays, a

1875   Confederate veteran and planter. Congressman Caldwell, also reelected, and five of six new Representatives were all Democrats: Taul Bradford, Talladega attorney; William H. Forney, Jacksonville attorney; Goldsmith W. Hewitt, Birmingham attorney; Burwell B. Lewis, Tuscaloosa businessman; and Jeremiah N. Williams, Clayton attorney. The eighth Representative was a black, Republican Jeremiah Haralson of Selma.

1876   *August*. Democrats reelected Governor Houston by almost 2-to-1 majority over Noahiah Woodruff, last Republican candidate to make serious bid for the office. Republicans in each house of state legislature were reduced to small minority and virtually disappeared by 1880. Complete Democratic sweep of Congressional delegation. John T. Morgan Confederate army veteran and lawyer of Selma, elected to seat of Senator Goldthwaite.

State debt commission fixed Alabama's state debt, after Reconstruction, at $30,017,563. By program of refunding through 20-year bonds, commission brought state back to solvency by 1879.

1877   *January 24*. Cullman County created and named for Johann G. Cullman, German emigrant who had introduced largescale development of settlements of Germans under North Alabama Land Company.

February 8. Sanford County renamed Lamar County for Lucius Q. C. Lamar, Mississippi Confederate veteran and statesman, who led reconciliation movement in Congress.

October 1. New public school system, on segregated basis but providing for statewide education for all races, went into effect.

October 15. Congressmen Forney, Hewitt and

1877   Williams reelected and took seats. New
                Representatives: William W. Garth, Huntsville, and
                Hilary A. Herbert, Montgomery, both Confederate
                veterans; James T. Jones, Demopolis, judge advocate
                general in the Confederate army; Robert F. Ligon,
                Tuskegee, who had been lieutenant governor in 1874
                (an office created by constitution of 1868); and
                Charles M. Shelley of Selma. Shelley's seat was
                unsuccessfully contested, the first of ten Alabama
                Congressional seats contested during next two
                decades as remnants of old political machines
                maneuvered for return to power.

1878   Alabama Greenback Party, although not strong
                enough to put forward its own slate, supported
                selected candidates of major parties in state and
                Congressional elections. William M. Lowe of
                Huntsville won seat in Congress for next year with
                Greenback support.

                November 28. Rufus W. Cobb, Shelby County,
                elected governor. Cobb, a railroad attorney, had
                framed much of Governor Houston's refunding
                program in 1876.

1879   *February 12.* Alabama State Bar Association
                incorporated.

                March 4. Congressmen Herbert and Shelley reelected;
                new Representatives included William M. Lowe of
                Huntsville, who had combined Democratic and
                Greenbacker support; Burwell B. Lewis, Tuscaloosa
                coal and iron dealer, who resigned October 1, 1880;
                William J. Sanford, Opelika attorney; and two
                members of the state house of representatives
                Thomas H. Herndon of Mobile and Thomas Williams
                of Wetumpka.

                March 18. Houston, who had won election to Senator
                Spencer's seat, was formally sworn in. He died

1879   December 31.

1880   Population listed by decennial census at 1,262,505.

January 15. Luke Pryor, Athens, appointed to seat of late Senator Houston. Pryor was "elder statesman," member of state house of representatives in 1855 and 1856.

June 25. Greenback Party held convention at Montgomery and nominated its own slate for state offices. That fall it elected five members of state house of representatives and successfully contested two Congressional seats in favor of Congressmen Lowe and James Q. Smith.

December 6. James L. Pugh, Eufala, elected to fill out Senator Houston's term. A member of Congress 1859-61 and of the Confederate Congress 1861-65, he had also been a leader in 1875 constitutional convention.

December 8. Newton N. Clements, speaker of state house of representatives, took seat of Congressman Lewis.

1881   *February 10*. Tuskegee Institute founded.

February 21. State railroad commission created to regulate rates and rebates.

December 5. Congressmen Forney, Herbert, Herndon, Shelley and Williams reelected previous fall and now seated. New Representatives included former Congressman Goldsmith W. Hewitt, Confederate veteran William C. Oates of Abbeville, and Mexican War and Confederate veteran Joseph Wheeler.

1882   *June 3*. William M. Lowe, Greenback candidate who contested Wheeler's election, seated in his place; died

1882 August 12 and Wheeler reappointed. This was one of continuing series of contests reflecting power struggles within state political structure.

 December 1. Edward Asbury O'Neal, Lauderdale County, elected on now-standard "Bourbon" platform of strict economy.

1883 *December 3.* Congressmen Forney, Herbert, Hewitt, Oates, Shelley and Williams, elected previous year, were seated. Congressman Herndon was also reelected but died before session began. He was succeeded by James T. Jones, former Confederate officer in Judge Advocate General's Corps. Eighth Representative was ex-Congressman Luke Pryor.

1885 First street railway opened in Montgomery.

 January 9. Judge George H. Craig, Selma, successfully contested and won seat held by Congressman Shelley.

 November. Rivers and harbors meeting at Tuscaloosa reflected concern of Alabama and neighboring states at steady decline of water commerce.

 December 7. Congressmen Forney, Jones, Herbert and Oates reelected. New Representatives: Alexander C. Davidson, Uniontown planter; John M. Martin, law professor of Tuscaloosa; Thomas W. Sadler of Prattville and Joseph Wheeler of Wheeler, both Confederate veterans.

1886 *July 11.* Alabama Prohibition Party nominated first state ticket.

 December 1. Thomas Seay, Hale County, "dark horse" candidate, won race for governor as party leaders split their support for major candidates.

1887 *December 5.* Congressmen Davidson, Forney,

1887 Herbert, Jones, Oates and Wheeler, reelected in 1886, took seats. New Representatives included John H. Bankhead of Fayette, planter and founder of political dynasty, and James E. Cobb of Tuskegee, Confederate veteran and jurist.

December 14. Alabama bar adopted code of professional ethics, first in nation, later to be widely copied.

1888 *March 8.* First Alabama steel rolled at Bessemer.

December 8. Thirteen persons killed in riot at Birmingham.

1889 *February 28.* Pensions authorized for disabled Confederate veterans.

December 2. Congressmen reelected in 1888 included Bankhead, Cobb, Forney, Herbert, Oates and Wheeler. New Representatives, who successfully defended contested elections, were Richard H. Clarke of Mobile and Louis W. Turpin of Newbern.

1890 Population of state reached 1,513,017.

June 4. John V. McDuffie of Hayneville, Republican political leader and postwar probate judge, contested and won Congressman Turpin's seat.

December 1. Thomas Goode Jones of Montgomery elected governor. A leader of moderates and conservatives in the state, Jones was supported as a coalition candidate against rising threat of Populists and Farmer's Alliance party.

1891 *December 7.* Congressmen Bankhead, Clarke, Cobb, Forney, Herbert, Oates and Wheeler reelected. George Hearst, a new Representative, died before he could take office and ex-Congressman Turpin was elected to

1891   succeed him.

1892   Alabama Polytechnic Institute became coeducational.

1893   *March 6.* Hilary A. Herbert took office as Secretary
            of Navy under President Grover Cleveland.

            August 7. Alabama was entitled to nine
            Representatives under new census and in fall of 1892
            had reelected six: Congressmen Bankhead, Clarke,
            Cobb, Oates, Turpin and Wheeler. Three new
            Representatives were William H. Denson of Gadsden
            and Jesse F. Stallings of Greenville, prominent
            political leaders, and Gaston A. Robbins of Selma,
            prominent local attorney.

1894   *December 1.* Veteran Congressman William C. Oates
            elected governor, having been drafted as strongest
            candidate to keep Populist threat in check.

            December 3. George P. Harrison of Opelika,
            Confederate veteran and active political leader in
            state, elected to Congressman Oates' seat.

1895   *February 16.* Legislature approved new state flag,
            embodying elements of Confederate flag, with red St.
            Andrew's cross on white field.

            December 2. Congressmen Bankhead, Clarke, Cobb,
            Harrison, Robbins, Stallings, Wheeler reelected
            previous fall, took seats. New Representatives
            included Populist Milford W. Howard of Fort Payne
            and Oscar W. Underwood of Birmingham. Senator
            Morgan reelected.

1896   *March 13.* William F. Aldrich, Republican
            industrialist, successfully contested seat of
            Congressman Robbins.

            April 22. Albert T. Goodwyn, Confederate veteran,

1896

planter and member of state legislature, successfully contested seat of Congressman Cobb. These were further chapters in history of vigorous political struggles between local party factions of this period.

June 9. Truman H. Aldrich, brother of William F. Aldrich and vice-president of Tennessee Coal, Iron & Railroad Co., successfully contested seat of Congressman Underwood. Widespread charges of corruption in 1894 elections, repeated in 1896, led to charges of machine control of ballot counting by which regular Democrats counted out Republican, Populist and Jeffersonian Democratic candidates.

December 1. Joseph Fortney Johnson, veteran political leader who sometimes inclined toward Populism, won election as governor.

1897

March 15. Edmund W. Pettus, lawyer and former jurist, elected to succeed Senator Pugh previous fall, took his seat. In new Congress, only four incumbents were returned -- Bankhead, Howard, Stallings and Wheeler, although Congressman Underwood, unseated previous spring, won another term. New Representatives: Henry D. Clayton, U.S. District Attorney; William Brewer, planter and state legislator; Thomas W. Plowman, banker; and George W. Taylor, former judge.

July 24. First open hearth steel manufactured in state.

1898

University of Alabama became coeducational for all courses, some departments having admitted women since 1890.

February 9. William F. Aldrich again contested a seat, this time of Congressman Plowman, and was seated in his place.

1899   *December 4.* New Congressional delegation reflected final triumph of regular party; Representatives Bankhead, Brewer, Clayton, Stallings, Taylor, Underwood and Wheeler reelected, and ex-Congressman Robbins was elected to new term. Only newcomer was John L. Burnett, attorney and member of the state legislature.

1900   State population listed in census at 1,828,697.

       March 8. For third time William F. Aldrich successfully contested for Congressional seat, and for second time Congressman Robbins was ousted.

       December 1. William Dorsey Jelks became acting governor in course of Governor Johnston's vigorous campaign for John T. Morgan's Senate seat. Johnston, a former political protege of Morgan, led a protest movement against the proposal for a new constitutional convention which was intended to reduce Negro voting to a virtual disfranchisement.

       December 3. Former judge William Richardson took seat of former Congressman Wheeler, who had resigned.

       December 21. William James Samford, candidate of anti-Johnston forces, was elected governor but died the following June. Seriousness of his illness at time of election prompted constitutional convention to revive office of lieutenant governor, originally established in "carpetbag" constitution of 1868.

1901   *April 23.* Proposal for new constitutional convention carried by 70,305 to 45,505.

       May 21. Constitutional convention opened at Montgomery.

       June 11. William Dorsey Jelks succeeded late

1901   Governor Samford.

September 3. Draft of new constitution completed.
Movement for new constitution coincided with
similar efforts in other Southern states, primarily
aimed at disfranchising Negro and illiterate poor
whites and consolidating conservative control of state
political structure. Distrust of legislature, bred by
Populist uprising of previous decade, led to great
increase in wordage of new constitution,
incorporating many statutory regulations of
governmental processes so as to insulate them from
legislative reform.

November 11. New state constitution approved, 108,
613-81, 734.

December 2. New Congressional delegation, elected
previous fall, took seats. Reelected members included
Congressmen Bankhead, Burnett, Clayton,
Richardson, Taylor and Underwood. New members
included Ariosto A. Wiley, veteran state legislator,
Sydney J. Bowie, ardent advocate of new
constitution, and Charles W. Thompson, banker.

1903   *January 3.* Governor Jelks began second term.

February 9. Houston County created from parts of
Dale, Greene and Henry Counties and named for
Congressman George S. Houston.

November 9. Entire Alabama delegation reelected and
took seats in new Congress, evidence of effectiveness
of control of political organization of state under new
constitution.

1904   *April 25.* Dr. Russell McWhorter Cunningham named
acting governor.

December 5. J. Thomas Heflin sworn into seat of

1904   Congressman Thompson, deceased.

1905   *December 4.* Entire Congressional delegation, elected previous fall, took seats in new Congress.

1907   *January 14.* Braxton Bragg Comer, influential planter and business leader, became governor.

            March 12. General juvenile court law enacted, following establishment in Mobile of first special juvenile court in state.

            December 2. Congressmen Burnett, Clayton, Heflin, Richardson, Taylor, Underwood and Wiley reelected, and took seats in new Congress. New Representatives: William H. Craig of Selma and Richard P. Hobson of Greensboro.

            December 3. Joseph F. Johnston formally seated in place of late Senator Pettus.

1908   *January 13.* John H. Bankhead inducted into seat of late Senator Morgan.

            December 7. Oliver A. Wiley succeeded to seat of his brother, Ariosto, deceased.

1909   *March 15.* All of incumbent Congressional delegation reelected except Congressman Wiley, who retired and was succeeded by S. Hubert Dent, Jr. of Montgomery.

1910   State population listed at 2,138,093.

1911   *January 17.* Emmett O'Neal, Lauderdale, elected governor.

            April 4. All of Congressional delegation reelected and seated except Congressman Craig, who was succeeded by Fred L. Blackmon of Anniston.

1913   *April 7.* All of Congressional delegation reelected; a
                tenth seat was declared open at large, and John W.
                Abercrombie of Tuscaloosa was elected.

                August 12. Congressman Clayton appointed to seat of
                Senator Johnston, deceased, but withdrew from
                consideration at request of President Wilson, who
                favored Congressman Underwood.

                November 17. Frank P. Glass was second appointee
                to Johnston's seat, but following February 14 a
                Senate resolution declared his credentials invalid,
                since the appointment had come after ratification of
                Sixteenth Amendment providing for popular election
                of Senators.

1914   *May 19.* Christopher C. Harris of Decatur elected to
                seat of Congressman Richardson, deceased.

                May 22. Frank S. White, duly elected to fill out
                Johnston's Senate term, formally seated.

                July 16. William O. Mulkey of Geneva elected to fill
                seat of Congressman Clayton, resigned.

1915   "Bone dry" prohibition went into effect in state,
                result of long term campaign of prohibitionists
                currently resulting in numerous state laws preparing
                way for national amendment.

                January 18. Charles Henderson of Pike County,
                banker and businessman, became governor.

                December 6. Congressman Underwood seated as
                successor to Senator White. Congressmen
                Abercrombie, Blackmon, Burnett, Dent and Heflin
                had been reelected; new Representatives now seated
                included Edward B. Almon, Tuscumbia, Oscar L.
                Grey, Butler, George Huddleston, Birmingham,
                William B. Oliver, Tuscaloosa and Henry B. Steagall,

1915   Ozark.

1916   Power and nitrate plant at Muscle Shoals authorized
            under general preparedness program of national
            government.

1917   *April 2.* Entire Congressional delegation reseated
            except Congressman Abercrombie, who was replaced
            by William B. Bankhead of Jasper.

            August 14. Fourth Alabama regiment became 167th
            Inf., U.S. Army – part of famed Rainbow Division in
            first World War.

1918   Program of workmen's compensation adopted in
            state.

1919   *January 20.* Thomas Erby Kilby of Calhoun County,
            industrialist and political leader, became governor.

            May 19. All of Congressional delegation reseated
            except Congressman Grey, succeeded by John
            McDuffie of Monroeville.

            October 13. Lilius B. Rainey of Gadsden elected to
            succeed late Congressman Burnett.

1920   New census showed state population of 2,348,174.

            March 15. Braxton Bragg Comer appointed to seat of
            Senator John Bankhead, deceased.

            December 6. Congressman Heflin elected to
            remainder of Senator Bankhead's term.

            December 29. William B. Bowling of Lafayette
            elected to fill seat of former Congressman Heflin.

1921   *June 27.* Lamar Jeffers of Anniston elected to seat of
            Congressman Blackmon, deceased.

1921   *April 1.* All of Congressional delegation reseated except Congressman Dent, who was replaced by John R. Tyson of Montgomery.

1923   *January 15.* William Woodward Brandon, Tuscaloosa County, attorney, jurist and political leader, became governor.

                 December 3. All of Congressional delegation returned to new Congress, except Congressman Rainey, who was succeeded by Miles C. Allgood of Allgood, and Congressman Tyson, deceased, who was succeeded by Lister Hill of Montgomery.

1925   *May 18.* First radio broadcasting station in state, WBRC, came on air in Birmingham.

                 December 7. All of Congressional delegation reelected.

1927   *January 17.* Bibb Graves of Montgomery County, attorney and popular political figure, became governor.

                 September 6. Yellowhammer designated as state bird.

                 December 5. Hugo L. Black of Birmingham seated in former place of Senator Underwood. All of Congressional delegation reelected.

1928   *June 30.* System of leasing convict labor abolished by statute.

                 December 3. LaFayette L. Patterson of Alexander City elected to replace Congressman Bowling, who had been appointed a judge.

1929   *April 15.* Entire Congressional delegation reseated for new Congress.

1930 Latest census: 2,646,248 population.

1931 *January 19.* Benjamin Meek Miller of Camden County, former justice of state supreme court, became governor.

    December 7. John H. Bankhead, 2d, seated as successor to Senator Heflin. All of Congressional delegation reelected.

1932 *March 21.* Hurricane rips through state, killing 315 persons.

1933 *March 9.* Congressional delegation reduced to nine; Congressman Pattersons' seat eliminated. Congressman Almon died June 22 and Archibald H. Carmichael of Tuscumbia was elected in his place.

1935 *January 14.* Governor Graves began second term.

    January 3. Seven Congressmen returned to this Congress; Congressmen Jeffers and Allgood replaced by Sam Hibbs of Selma and Joe Starnes of Guntersville.

    August 12. Frank J. Boykin of Mobile elected to seat of Congressmen McDuffie, who had been appointed a federal judge.

1936 *June 4.* Congressman Bankhead elected Speaker of House of Representatives.

1937 *January 5.* Congressmen Bankhead, Boykin, Hill, Hobbs, Starnes and Steagell returned. New Representatives included Pete Jarman of Livingston, Luther Patrick of Birmingham and John J. Sparkman of Huntsville.

    August 18. Senator Black nominated to be a Justice of United States Supreme Court.

1937   *August 20.* Mrs. Dixie Bibb Graves appointed to former Senate seat of Justice Black.

1938   *January 11.* Congressman Hill appointed to Black's seat upon resignation of Mrs. Graves.

June 14. George M. Grant of Troy appointed to Congressman Hill's seat but not sworn in as Congress had adjourned.

1939   *January 3.* All of Congressional delegation returned. Speaker Bankhead died September 15, 1940.

January 17. Frank M. Dixon of Jefferson County elected governor.

1940   Current census: 2,832,961 population.

November 11. Zadok L. Weatherford of Red Bay elected to seat of late Speaker Bankhead.

1941   *January 3.* All of Congressional delegation returned, except for Congressman Weatherford, replaced by Walter W. Bankhead of Jasper.

July 3. Carter Manasco of Jasper elected to seat of Congressman Bankhead, resigned.

1942   **?** *November.* Alabama voted Republican for President (Eisenhower), first time since Reconstruction.

1943   *January 6.* All of Congressional delegation returned except Congressman Patrick, replaced by John P. Newsome of Birmingham.

January 19. Chauncey Sparks of Barbour County became governor.

1944   *March 20.* George W. Andrews elected to seat of Congressman Steagall, deceased.

1945   *January 3.* All of Congressional delegation returned
              except Congressman Newsome, replaced by Albert
              Rains of Gadsden.

1946   *June 20.* George R. Swift of Atmore appointed to
              seat of Senator Bankhead, deceased.

1947   *January 3.* Congressman Sparkman elected to seat of
              Senator Bankhead and formally seated. Seven
              Congressmen returned; Robert E. Jones, Jr. of
              Scottsboro and Laurie C. Battle of Birmingham
              replaced Congressman Patrick.

              January 14. James E. Folsom became governor.

1949   *January 3.* Seven Congressmen returned;
              Congressmen Jarman and Manasco replaced by Carl
              A. Elliott of Jasper and Edward deGraffenreid of
              Tuscaloosa.

1950   Current census figures: 3,061,743.

1951   *January 3.* Eight Congressmen returned; Congressman
              Hobbs replaced by Kenneth A. Roberts of Piedmont.

              January 12. Gordon Persons elected governor.

1953   *January 3.* Eight Congressmen returned; Congressmen
              deGraffenreid replaced by Armistead I. Selden, Jr. of
              Greensboro.

1955   *January 5.* Eight Congressmen returned; Congressman
              Battle replaced by ex-Congressman George
              Huddleston, Jr. of Birmingham.

              January 15. Governor Folsom began second term.

1956   Congress created Horseshoe Bend National Military
              Park.

1957   *January 3*. Entire Congressional delegation returned.

1959   *January 7*. Entire Congressional delegation returned.

      January 12. John Patterson became governor.

1960   Census figures: 3,266,740.

      September 8. George C. Marshall Space Flight Center dedicated at Huntsville.

      November. Alabama cast 6 electoral votes for Senator Harry F. Byrd of Virginia, 5 electoral votes for John F. Kennedy.

1961   *January 3*. Entire Congressional delegation reelected.

      May. So-called "freedom rides" of integrationists provoked outbreaks of violence in several Alabama cities. U.S. Department of Justice sent number of federal marshals into state to protect riders.

1963   *January 3*. Alabama lost one Congressional seat, held by Representative Boykin. Remaining incumbents returned.

      January 10. George C. Wallace became governor.

1964   *June 11*. Three Negro students enrolled at University of Alabama over vigorous local protest. President Kennedy nationalized Alabama guard units which "regretfully" requested Governor Wallace to desist from personally barring entry.

      November. Alabama cast its electoral votes for Republican Presidential candidate Barry Goldwater.

1965   *January 3*. New Congressional delegation reflected Goldwater impact on previous fall elections: Three incumbent Democrats (Congressman George

1965   Andrews, Jones and Selden) returned with five new
            Republicans: W. Jack Edwards, Mobile; William L.
            Dickinson, Montgomery; Glenn Andrews, Anniston;
            John H. Buchanan, Birmingham; James D. Martin,
            Gadsden.

1967   *January 10.* Mrs. George C. (Lurleen) Wallace
            inaugurated as governor, her husband continuing as
            "advisor."

            January 10. Congressmen George Andrews,
            Buchanan, Dickinson, Edwards, Jones and Selden
            reelected. Democratic majority in delegation restored
            with election of Bill Nickols, Sylacauga, and Tom
            Bevill, Jasper.

1968   *November.* Alabama voted for George Wallace for
            President; running on third-party ticket, Wallace
            received 9,825,459 popular votes in the country at
            large, and 45 electoral votes.

            Albert P. Brewer, lieutenant governor, succeeded Mrs.
            Lurleen Wallace, deceased.

1970   Census figures: 3,444,165.

BIOGRAPHICAL DIRECTORY

The selected list of governors, United States Senators and Members of the House of Representatives for Alabama, 1819-1970, includes all persons listed in the Chronology for whom basic biographical data was readily available. Older biographical sources are frequently in conflict on certain individuals, and in such cases the source most commonly cited by later authorities was preferred.

ABERCROMBIE, James
  b. Hancock Co., Ga., 1795
  d. Pensacola, Fla., July 2, 1861
  U. S. Representative, 1851-55
ABERCROMBIE, John W.
  b. St. Clair Co., Ala., May 17, 1866
  d. Montgomery, Ala., July 2, 1940
  U. S. Representative, 1913-17
ALDRICH, Thomas H.
  b. Palmyra, N. Y., Oct. 17, 1848
  d. Birmingham, Ala., Apr. 28, 1932
  U. S. Representative, 1896-97
ALDRICH, William F.
  b. Palmyra, N. Y., Mar. 11, 1853
  d. Birmingham, Ala., Oct. 30, 1925
  U. S. Representative, 1897-97, 1898-99,
      1900-01
ALMON, Edward B.
  b. Lawrence Co., Ala., Apr. 18, 1860
  d. Washington, D. C., June 22, 1933
  U. S. Representative, 1915-33
ALSTON, William J.
  b. Milledgeville, Ga., Dec. 31, 1800
  d. Marengo Co., Ala., June 10, 1876
  U. S. Representative, 1849-51
BANKHEAD, John H.
  b. Lamar Co., Ala., Sept. 13, 1842
  d. Washington, D. C., Mar. 1, 1920
  U. S. Representative, U. S. Senator
BANKHEAD, John H., 2d
  b. Lamar Co., Ala., July 8, 1872
  d. Bethesda, Md., June 12, 1946
  U. S. Senator, 1930-46

BANKHEAD, William B.
 b. Lamar Co., Ala., Apr. 12, 1874
 d. Washington, D. C., Sept. 25, 1940
 U. S. Representative, 1917-40
BAYLOR, Robert E. B.
 b. Lincoln Co., Ky., May 10, 1793
 d. Washington Co., Tex., Jan. 6, 1874
 U. S. Representative, 1829-31
BELSER, James E.
 b. Charleston, S. C., Dec. 22, 1805
 d. Montgomery, Ala., Jan. 16, 1859
 U. S. Representative, 1843-45
BIBB, Thomas
 b. Amelia Co., Va., 1784
 d. Alabama, 1838
 Governor of Alabama, 1820-21
BIBB, William Wyatt
 b. Prince Edward Co., Va., Oct. 1, 1780
 d. Huntsville, Ala., July 10, 1820
 U. S. Representative (Ga.), 1807-13
 U. S. Senator (Ga.), 1813-16
 Territorial governor of Alabama, 1817-19
 First governor of Alabama, 1819-20
BLACK, Hugo L.
 b. Clay Co., Ala., Feb. 27, 1886
 d. Washington, D. C., Sept.　, 1971
 U. S. Senator, 1927-37
 Associate Justice, U. S. Supreme Court,
  1937-71
BLACKMON, Fred L.
 b. Polk Co., Ga., Sept. 15, 1873
 d. Polk Co., Fla., Feb. 8, 1921
 U. S. Representative, 1911-21
BOWDON, Franklin W.
 b. Chester Dist., S. C., Feb. 17, 1817
 d. Henderson, Tex., June 8, 1857
 U. S. Representative, 1846-51
BOWIE, Sydney J.
 b. Talladega, Ala., July 26, 1865

d. Birmingham, Ala., May 7, 1928
U. S. Representative, 1901–07
BOWLING, William B.
  b. Calhoun Co., Ala., Sept. 24, 1870
  d. Lafayette, Ala., Dec. 27, 1946
  U. S. Representative, 1920–28
BRADFORD, Taul
  b. Talladega, Ala., Jan. 20, 1835
  d. Talladega, Ala., Oct. 28, 1883
  U. S. Representative, 1875–77
BRAGG, John
  b. Warrenton, N. C., Jan. 14, 1806
  d. Mobile, Ala., Aug. 10, 1878
  U. S. Representative, 1851–53
BREWER, Willis
  b. Sumter Co., Ala., Mar. 15, 1844
  d. Montgomery, Ala., Oct. 30, 1912
  U. S. Representative, 1897–1901
BROMBERG, Frederick G.
  b. New York, N. Y., Jan. 19, 1837
  d. Mobile, Ala., Sept. 4, 1930
  U. S. Representative, 1873–75
BUCK, Alfred E.
  b. Foxcroft, Me., Feb. 7, 1832
  d. Tokyo, Japan, Dec. 4, 1902
  U. S. Representative, 1869–71
  Minister to Japan, 1897–1902
BUCKLEY, Charles W.
  b. Otsego Co., N. Y., Feb. 18, 1835
  d. Montgomery, Ala., Dec. 4, 1906
  U. S. Representative, 1868–73
BURNETT, John L.
  b. Cherokee Co., Ala., Jan. 20, 1854
  d. Gadsden, Ala., May 13, 1919
  U. S. Representative, 1899–1919
CALDWELL, John H.
  b. Huntsville, Ala., Apr. 4, 1826
  d. Jacksonville, Ala., Sept. 4, 1902
  U. S. Representative, 1873–77

CALLIS, John B.
   b. Fayetteville, N. C., Jan. 3, 1828
   d. Lancaster, Wisc., Sept. 24, 1898
   U. S. Representative, 1868-69
CARMICHAEL, Archibald H.
   b. Dale Co., Ala., June 17, 1864
   d. Tuscumbia, Ala., July 15, 1947
   U. S. Representative, 1933-37
CHAMBERS, Henry H.
   b. Lunenburg Co., Va., Oct. 1, 1790
   d. Lunenburg Co., Va., Feb. 24, 1826
   U. S. Senator, 1825-26
CHAPMAN, Reuben
   b. Bowling Green, Va., July 15, 1799
   d. Huntsville, Ala., May 16, 1892
   Governor of Alabama, 1847-49
   U. S. Representative, 1835-47
   Confederate Minister to France, 1862-65
CLARKE, Richard H.
   b. Marengo Co., Ala., Feb. 9, 1843
   d. St. Louis, Mo., Sept. 26, 1906
   U. S. Representative, 1889-97
CLAY, Clement Comer
   b. Halifax Co., Va., Dec. 17, 1789
   d. Huntsville, Ala., Sept. 9, 1886
   Chief Justice of Alabama, 1820-23
   U. S. Representative, 1829-35
   Governor of Alabama, 1836-37
   U. S. Senator, 1837-41
CLAY, Clement Claiborne, Jr.
   b. Huntsville, Ala., Dec. 13, 1816
   d. Madison Co., Ala., Jan. 3, 1882
   U. S. Senator, 1853-61
   Confederate Senator, 1861-63
CLAYTON, Henry D.
   b. Barbour Co., Ala., Feb. 10, 1857
   d. Montgomery, Ala., Dec. 21, 1929
   U. S. Representative, 1897-1914

CLEMENS, Jeremiah
  b. Huntsville, Ala., Dec. 28, 1814
  d. Huntsville, Ala., May 21, 1865
  U. S. Senator, 1849-53
CLEMENTS, Newton N.
  b. Tuscaloosa Co., Ala., Dec. 23, 1837
  d. Tuscaloosa Co., Ala., Feb. 20, 1900
  U. S. Representative, 1880-81
CLOPTON, David
  b. Putnam C., Ga., Sept. 29, 1820
  d. Montgomery, Ala., Feb. 5, 1892
  U. S. Representative, 1859-61
  Confederate Representative, 1862-64
  Justice, Supreme Court of Alabama, 1884-92
COBB, James E.
  b. Upson Co., Ga., Oct. 5, 1835
  d. San Miguel Co., N. M., June 2, 1903
  U. S. Representative, 1887-96
COBB, Williamson R. W.
  b. Rhea Co., Tenn., June 8, 1807
  d. Bellefontaine, Ala., Nov. 1, 1864
  U. S. Representative, 1847-61
COLLIER, Henry W.
  b. Lunenburg Co., Va., Jan. 17, 1801
  d. Florence, Ala., Aug. 28, 1855
  Chief Justice of Alabama, 1837-49
  Governor of Alabama, 1849-53
COMER, Braxton Bragg
  b. Mobile Co., Ala., Nov. 7, 1848
  d. Birmingham, Ala., Aug. 15, 1927
  Governor of Alabama, 1907-11
  U. S. Senator, Mar. - Nov., 1920
COTTRELL, James L. F.
  b. King William Co., Va., Aug. 25, 1808
  d. Cedar Keys, Fla, Sept. 7, 1885
  U. S. Representative, 1846-47
CRABB, George W.
  b. Botetourt Co., Va., Feb. 22, 1804
  d. Philadelphia, Pa., Aug. 15, 1846

U. S. Representative, 1838–41
CRAIG, George H.
  b. Dallas Co., Ala., Dec. 25, 1845
  d. Selma, Ala., Jan. 26, 1923
  U. S. Representative, Jan. – Mar., 1885
CRAIG, William B.
  b. Dallas Co., Ala., Nov. 2, 1877
  d. Selma, Ala., Nov. 27, 1925
  U. S. Representative, 1907–11
CROWELL, John
  b. Halifax Co., N. C., Sept. 18, 1780
  d. Ft. Mitchell, Ala., June 25, 1846
  Territorial Delegate (Ala.), 1818–19
  First U. S. Representative, 1819–21
CUNNINGHAM, Russell McWhorter
  b. Mt. Hope, Ala., Aug. 25, 1855
  d. Birmingham, Ala., 1922
  Acting Governor of Alabama, 1904–05
CURRY, Jabez L. M.
  b. Lincoln Co., Ga., June 5, 1825
  d. Asheville, N. C., Feb. 12, 1903
  U. S. Representative, 1857–61
  Confederate Representative, 1861–63
  U. S. Minister to Spain, 1885–87
DARGAN, Edmund S.
  b. Montgomery Co., N. C., Apr. 15, 1805
  d. Mobile, Ala., Nov. 22, 1879
  U. S. Representative, 1845–47
  Chief Justice of Alabama, 1849–52
DAVIDSON, Alexander C.
  b. Charlotte, N. C., Dec. 26, 1826
  d. Uniontown, Ala., Nov. 6, 1897
  U. S. Representative, 1885–89
DELLET, James
  b. Camden, N. J., Feb. 18, 1788
  d. Claiborne, Ala., Dec. 21, 1848
  U. S. Representative, 1839–45
DENSON, William H.
  b. Russell Co., Ala., Mar. 4, 1846

d. Birmingham, Ala., Sept. 26, 1906
U. S. Representative, 1893-95
DENT, S. Hubert, Jr.
b. Barbour Co., Ala., Aug. 16, 1869
d. Montgomery, Ala., Oct. 6, 1938
U₂ₐS. Representative, 1909-1920
DOWDELL, James F.
b. Jasper Co., Ala., Nov. 26, 1818
d. Lee Co., Ala., Sept. 6, 1871
U. S. Representative, 1853-59
DOX, Peter M.
b. Geneva, N. Y., Sept. 11, 1813
d. Huntsville, Ala., Apr. 2, 1891
U. S. Representative, 1869-73
FITZPATRICK, Benjamin F.
b. Greene Co., Ga., June 30, 1802
d. Wetumpka, Ala., Nov. 25, 1869
Governor of Alabama, 1841-45
U. S. Senator, 1848-49, 1853-61
FORNEY, William H.
b. Lincoln Co., N. C., Nov. 9, 1823
d. Jacksonville, Ala., Jan. 16, 1894
U. S. Representative, 1875-93
GARTH, William W.
b. Morgan Co., Ala., Oct. 28, 1828
d. Huntsville, Ala., Feb. 25, 1912
U. S. Representative, 1877-79
GAYLE, John
b. Sumter Dist., S. C., Sept. 11, 1792
d. Mobile, Ala., July 28, 1859
Associate Justice, Alabama Supreme Court,
1823
Governor of Alabama, 1831-35
U. S. Representative, 1847-49
GOLDTHWAITE, George T.
b. Boston, Mass., Dec. 10, 1809
d. Tuscaloosa, Ala., Mar. 18, 1879
Chief Justice of Alabama, 1856
U. S. Representative, 1871-77

GOODWYN, Albert T.
   b. Montgomery Co., Ala., Dec. 17, 1842
   d. Birmingham, Ala., July 2, 1931
   U. S. Representative, 1896-97
GRAY, Oscar L.
   b. in Mississippi, July 2, 1865
   d. Shreveport, La., Jan. 2, 1936
   U. S. Representative, 1915-19
HANDLEY, William A.
   b. Heard Co., Ga., Dec. 15, 1834
   d. Roanoke, Ala., June 23, 1909
   U. S. Representative, 1871-73
HARALSON, Jeremiah
   b. Muscogee Co., Ga., Apr. 1, 1846
   d. Denver, Colo., 1916
   U. S. Representative, 1875-77
HARRIS, Christopher C.
   b. Lawrence Co., Ala., Jan. 28, 1842
   d. Decatur, Ala., Dec. 28, 1935
   U. S. Representative, 1914-15
HARRIS, Sampson W.
   b. Elbert Co., Ga., Feb. 23, 1809
   d. Washington, D. C., Apr. 1, 1857
   U. S. Representative, 1847-57
HARRISON, George P.
   b. Savannah, Ga., Mar. 19, 1841
   d. Opelika, Ala., July 17, 1922
   U. S. Representative, 1894-97
HAUGHEY, Thomas
   b. Glasgow, Scotland, 1826
   d. Courtland, Ala., August 1869
   U. S. Representative, 1868-69
HAYS, Charles
   b. Greene Co., Ala., Feb. 2, 1834
   d. Greene Co., Ala., June 24, 1879
   U. S. Representative, 1869-77

HEFLIN, J. Thomas
    b. Randolph Co., Ala., Apr. 9, 1869
    d. Lafayette, Ala., Aug. 22, 1951
    U. S. Representative, 1904-20
    U. S. Senator, 1920-31
HEFLIN, Robert S.
    b. Morgan Co., Ga., Apr. 15, 1815
    d. Randolph Co., Ala., Jan. 24, 1901
    U. S. Representative, 1869-71
HERBERT, Hilary A.
    b. Laurence Co., S. C., Mar. 12, 1834
    d. Tampa, Fla., Mar. 5, 1919
    U. S. Representative, 1877-93
    Secretary of Navy, 1893-97
HERNDON, Thomas H.
    b. Hale Co., Ala., July 1, 1828
    d. Mobile, Ala., Mar. 28, 1883
    U. S. Representative, 1879-83
HEWITT, Goldsmith W.
    b. Jefferson Co., Ala., Feb. 14, 1834
    d. Birmingham, Ala., May 27, 1895
    U. S. Representative, 1875-79, 1881-85
HILLIARD, Henry W.
    b. Fayetteville, N. C., Aug. 4, 1808
    d. Atlanta, Ga., Dec. 17, 1892
    U. S. Representative, 1845-51
    U. S. Minister to Brazil, 1877-81
HOBBS, Sam F.
    b. Selma, Ala., Oct. 5, 1887
    d. Selma, Ala., May 31, 1952
    U. S. Representative, 1935-51
HOBSON, Richard P.
    b. Hale Co., Ala., Aug. 17, 1870
    d. New York, N. Y., Mar. 16, 1937
    U. S. Representative, 1907-15
HOUSTON, George Smith
    b. Williamson Co., Tenn., Jan. 17, 1808
    d. Athens, Ala., Dec. 31, 1879
    U. S. Representative, 1841-49, 1851-61

HOWARD, Milford W.
   b. Rome, Ga., Dec. 18, 1862
   d. Los Angeles, Calif., Dec. 28, 1937
   U. S. Representative, 1895-99
HUBBARD, David
   b. Bedford Co., Va., 1792
   d. Pte. Coupe, La., Jan. 20, 1874
   U. S. Representative, 1839-41, 1849-51
   Confederate Representative, 1861-63
HUDDLESTON, George
   b. Wilson Co., Tenn., Nov. 11, 1869
   d. Birmingham, Ala., Feb. 29, 1960
   U. S. Representative, 1915-37
INGE, Samuel
   b. Warren Co., N. C., Feb. 22, 1817
   d. San Francisco, Calif., June 10, 1868
   U. S. Representative, 1847-51
JARMAN, Pete
   b. Greenesboro, Ala., Oct. 31, 1892
   d. Washington, D. C., Feb. 17, 1955
   U. S. Representative, 1937-49
   U. S. Ambassador, 1949-53
JELKS, William Dorsey
   b. Russell Co., Ala., Nov. 7, 1855
   d. Birmingham, Ala., Dec. 13, 1931
   Governor of Alabama, 1901-07
JOHNSTON, Joseph Fortney
   b. Lincoln Co., N. C., Mar. 23, 1843
   d. Washington, D. C. Aug. 8, 1913
   Governor of Alabama, 1896-1900
   U. S. Senator, 1907-13
JONES, James T.
   b. Richmond, Va., July 20, 1832
   d. Demopolis, Ala., Feb. 15, 1895
   Confederate Judge Advocate General,
     1862-65
   U. S. Representative, 1877-79, 1883-89

JONES, Thomas Goode
 b. Macon, Ga., Nov. 26, 1844
 d. Montgomery, Ala., Apr. 28, 1914
 Governor of Alabama, 1890-94
KELLOGG, Francis W.
 b. Worthington, Mass., May 30, 1810
 d. Alliance, Ohio, Jan. 13, 1879
 U. S. Representative (Mich.), 1859-65
 U. S. Representative (Ala.), 1868-69
KELLY, William
 b. Tennessee, 1780
 d. New Orleans, La., 1832
 U. S. Senate, 1822-25
KILBY, Thomas Erby
 b. Lebanon, Tenn., July 9, 1865
 d. Anniston, Ala., Oct. 22, 1943
 Governor of Alabama, 1919-23
KING, William R.
 b. Sampson Co., N. C., Apr. 7, 1786
 d. Alabama, Apr. 18, 1853
 U. S. Representative (N.C.), 1811-16
 U. S. Senator (Ala.), 1819-44, 1848-52
 U. S. Minister to France, 1844-46
 U. S. Vice-President, Mar.-Apr., 1853
LAWLER, Joab
 b. Union Co., N. C., June 12, 1796
 d. Washington, D. C., May 8, 1838
 U. S. Representative, 1835-38
LEWIS, Burwell B.
 b. Montgomery, Ala., July 7, 1838
 d. Tuscaloosa, Ala., Oct. 11, 1885
 U. S. Representative, 1875-77, 1879-80
LEWIS, David Peter
 b. Charlotte Co., Va., 1820
 d. Huntsville, Ala., July 3, 1884
 Governor of Alabama, 1872-76
LEWIS, Dixon H.
 b. Dinwiddie Co., Va., Aug. 10, 1802
 d. New York, N. Y., Oct. 25, 1848

U. S. Representative, 1829-44
U. S. Senator, 1844-48
LIGON, Robert F.
  b. Watkinsville, Ga., Dec. 16, 1823
  d. Montgomery, Ala., Oct. 11, 1901
  Lt. Governor of Alabama, 1874
  U. S. Representative, 1877-79
LINDSAY, Robert Burns
  b. Dumfriesshire, Scotland, July 4, 1824
  d. Tuscumbia, Ala., 1902
  Governor of Alabama, 1870-71
LOWE, William M.
  b. Huntsville, Ala., June 12, 1842
  d. Huntsville, Ala., Oct. 12, 1882
  U. S. Representative, 1879-82
LYON, Francis S.
  b. Stokes Co., N. C., Feb. 25, 1800
  d. Demopolis, Ala., Dec. 31, 1882
  U. S. Representative, 1835-39
  Confederate Representative, 1862-65
MARDIS, Samuel W.
  b. Fayetteville, Tenn., June 12, 1800
  d. Talladega, Ala., Nov. 14, 1836
  U. S. Representative, 1831-35
MARTIN, John M.
  b. Limestone Co., Ala., Jan. 20, 1837
  d. Bowling Green, Ky., June 16, 1898
  U. S. Representative, 1885-87
MARTIN, Joshua Lanier
  b. Blount Co., Tenn., Dec. 5, 1799
  d. Tuscaloosa, Ala., Nov. 2, 1856
  U. S. Representative, 1835-39
  Governor of Alabama, 1845-47
McCONNELL, Felix G.
  b. Nashville, Tenn., Apr. 1, 1809
  d. Washington, D. C., Sept. 10, 1846
  U. S. Representative, 1843-46
McDUFFIE, John V.
  b. Monroe Co., Ala., Sept. 25, 1883

d. Mobile, Ala., Nov. 1, 1950
U. S. Representative, 1919-35
McKEE, John
  b. Rockbridge Co., Va., 1771
  d. Greene Co., Ala., Aug. 12, 1832
  U. S. Representative, 1823-29
McKINLEY, John
  b. Culpepper Co., Va., May 1, 1780
  d. Louisville, Ky., July 19, 1852
  U. S. Representative, 1833-35
  Associate Justice, U. S. Supreme Court,
    1837-52
MILLER, Benjamin Meek
  b. Wilcox Co., Ala., Mar. 13, 1864
  d. Selma, Ala., Feb. 6, 1944
  Justice, Alabama Supreme Court, 1920-26
  Governor of Alabama, 1930-34
MOORE, Andrew Barry
  b. Spartansburg, S. C., Mar. 7, 1807
  d. Marion Co., Ala., Apr. 5, 1873
  Governor of Alabama, 1857-61
MOORE, Gabriel
  b. Stokes Co., N. C., 1785
  d. Texas, June 9, 1845
  U. S. Representative, 1821-29
  Governor of Alabama, 1829-31
  U. S. Senator, 1831-37
MOORE, Samuel B.
  b. Franklin Co., Tenn., 1789
  d. Carrollton, Ala., Nov. 7, 1846
  Acting Governor of Alabama, 1831-33
MOORE, Sydenham
  b. Rutherford Co., Tenn., May 25, 1817
  d. Richmond, Va., May 31, 1862
  U. S. Representative, 1857-61
MORGAN, John T.
  b. Athens, Tenn., June 20, 1824
  d. Washington, D. C., June 11, 1907
  U. S. Senator, 1877-1907

MULKEY, William O.
  b. Pike Co., Ala., July 27, 1871
  d. Geneva, Ala., June 30, 1943
  U. S. Representative, 1914-15
MURPHY, John
  b. Columbia, N. C., 1786
  d. Clarke Co., Ala., Sept. 21, 1841
  Governor of Alabama, 1825-29
  U. S. Representative, 1833-35
NEWSOME, John P.
  b. Memphis, Tenn., Feb. 13, 1893
  d. Birmingham, Ala., Nov. 10, 1961
  U. S. Representative, 1943-45
NORRIS, Benjamin W.
  b. Monmouth, Me., Jan. 22, 1819
  d. Montgomery, Ala., Jan. 26, 1873
  U. S. Representative, 1868-69
OATES, William Calvin
  b. Pike Co., Ala., Nov. 30, 1835
  d. Montgomery, Ala., Sept. 9, 1910
  U. S. Representative, 1881-94
  Governor of Alabama, 1894-96
OLIVER, William B.
  b. Greene Co., Ala., May 23, 1867
  d. New Orleans, La., May 27, 1948
  U. S. Representative, 1915-37
O'NEAL, Edward Asbury
  b. Madison Co., Ala., Sept. 20, 1818
  d. Florence, Ala., Nov. 7, 1890
  Governor of Alabama, 1882-86
O'NEAL, Emmett
  b. Florence, Ala., Sept. 23, 1853
  d. Birmingham, Ala., Sept. 7, 1922
  Governor of Alabama, 1911-15
PARSONS, Lewis E.
  b. Broome Co., N. Y., Aug. 28, 1817
  d. Talladega, Ala., June 8, 1895
  Provisional governor, 1865-66

PATRICK, Luther
  b. Morgan Co., Ala., Jan. 23, 1894
  d. Birmingham, Ala., May 26, 1957
  U. S. Representative, 1937-43, 1945-47
PATTON, Robert Miller
  b. Monroe Co., Va., July 10, 1809
  d. Florence, Ala., Feb. 28, 1885
  Governor of Alabama, 1865-68
PAYNE, William W.
  b. Fauquier Co., Va., Jan. 2, 1807
  d. Warrenton, Va., Sept. 2, 1874
  U. S. Representative, 1841-47
PELHAM, Charles
  b. Person Co., N. C., Mar. 12, 1835
  d. Poulon, Ga., Jan. 18, 1908
  U. S. Representative, 1873-75
PETTUS, Edmund W.
  b. Limestone Co., Ala., July 6, 1821
  d. Madison Co., Ala., July 27, 1907
  U. S. Senator, 1897-1907
PHILLIPS, Philip
  b. Charleston, S. C., Dec. 13, 1807
  d. Washington, D. C., Jan. 14, 1884
  U. S. Representative, 1853-55
PICKENS, Israel
  b. Mecklenburg Co., N. C., Jan. 30, 1780
  d. Matanzas, Cuba, Apr. 24, 1827
  U. S. Representative (N.C.), 1811-17
  Governor of Alabama, 1821-25
  U. S. Senator, Feb.-Nov., 1826
PIERCE, Charles W.
  b. Benton, N. Y., Oct. 7, 1823
  d. Hastings, Fla., Feb. 18, 1907
  U. S. Representative, 1868-69
PLOWMAN, Thomas S.
  b. Talladega, Ala., June 8, 1843
  d. Talladega, Ala., July 26, 1919
  U. S. Representative, 1897-98

PRYOR, Luke
   b. Huntsville, Ala., July 5, 1820
   d. Athens, Ala., Aug. 5, 1900
   U. S. Senator, Jan.-Nov., 1880
   U. S. Representative, 1883-85
PUGH, James L.
   b. Burke Co., Ga., Dec. 12, 1820
   d. Washington, D. C., Mar. 9, 1907
   U. S. Representative, 1859-61
   Confederate Representative, 1861-65
   U. S. Senator, 1880-97
RAINEY, Lilius B.
   b. Tallapoosa Co., Ala., July 27, 1876
   d. Gadsden, Ala., Sept. 27, 1959
   U. S. Representative, 1919-23
RAPIER, James T.
   b. Lauderdale Co., Ala., Nov. 13, 1837
   d. Montgomery, Ala., May 31, 1883
   U. S. Representative, 1873-75
RICHARDSON, William
   b. Limestone Co., Ala., May 8, 1839
   d. Atlantic City, N. J., Mar. 31, 1914
   U. S. Representative, 1900-14
ROBBINS, Gaston A.
   b. Goldsboro, N. C., Sept. 26, 1858
   d. New York, N. Y., Feb. 22, 1902
   U. S. Representative, 1893-95, 1899-1900
SADLER, Thomas W.
   b. Franklin Co., Ala., Apr. 17, 1831
   d. Autauga Co., Ala., Oct. 29, 1896
   U. S. Representative, 1885-87
SAMFORD, William James
   b. Greenesville, Ga., Sept. 16, 1844
   d. Tuscaloosa, Ala., June 11, 1901
   U. S. Representative, 1879-81
   Governor of Alabama, 1900-01
SEAY, Thomas
   b. Greene Co., Ala., 1846
   d. Greensboro, Ala., Mar. 30, 1896

Governor of Alabama, 1886–90
SHEATS, Charles C.
   b. Walker Co., Ala., Apr. 10, 1839
   d. Morgan Co., Ala., May 27, 1904
   U. S. Representative, 1873–75
SHELLEY, Charles M.
   b. Sullivan Co., Tenn., Dec. 8, 1833
   d. Birmingham, Ala., Jan. 20, 1907
   U. S. Representative, 1882–85
SHERROD, William C.
   b. Lawrence Co., Ala., Aug. 17, 1835
   d. Wichita Falls, Tex., Mar. 24, 1919
   U. S. Representative, 1869–71
SHIELDS, Benjamin G.
   b. Abbeville, S. C., 1808
   d. Venezuela, Jan. 7, 1850
   U. S. Representative, 1841–43
   U. S. Charge d'affaires, Venezuela, 1845–50
SHORTER, John Gill
   b. Jasper Co., Ala., Apr. 23, 1818
   d. Eufala, Ala., May 29, 1872
   Governor of Alabama, 1861–63
SHORTER, Eli S.
   b. Jasper Co., Ala., Mar. 15, 1823
   d. Eufala, Ala., Apr. 29, 1879
   U. S. Representative, 1855–59
SLOSS, Joseph H.
   b. Somerville, Ala., Oct. 12, 1826
   d. Memphis, Tenn., Jan. 27, 1911
   U. S. Representative, 1871–75
SMITH, William Hugh
   b. Fayette Co., Ga., Apr. 26, 1826
   d. Birmingham, Ala., Jan. 1, 1899
   Governor of Alabama, 1868–70
SMITH, William Russell
   b. Russellville, Ky., Mar. 27, 1815
   d. Washington, D. C., Feb. 26, 1896
   U. S. Representative, 1851–57

SPENCER, George E.
   b. Jefferson Co., N. Y., Nov. 1, 1836
   d. Washington, D. C., Feb. 19, 1893
   U. S. Senator, 1868–79
STALLINGS, Jesse F.
   b. Butler Co., Ala., Apr. 4, 1856
   d. Birmingham, Ala., Mar. 18, 1928
   U. S. Representative, 1893–1901
STALLWORTH, James A.
   b. Conecuh Co., Ala., Apr. 7, 1822
   d. Conecuh Co., Ala., Aug. 31, 1861
   U. S. Representative, 1857–61
TAYLOR, George W.
   b. Montgomery Co., Ala., Jan. 16, 1849
   d. Rome, Ga., Dec. 21, 1932
   U. S. Representative, 1897–1915
THOMPSON, Charles W.
   b. Macon Co., Ala., Dec. 30, 1860
   d. Washington, D. C., Mar. 30, 1904
   U. S. Representative, 1901–04
TURNER, Benjamin S.
   b. Halifax Co., N. C., Mar. 17, 1825
   d. Selma, Ala., Mar. 21, 1894
   U. S. Representative, 1871–73
TURPIN, Louis W.
   b. Charlottesville, Va., Feb. 22, 1849
   d. Greensboro, Ala., Feb. 3, 1903
   U. S. Representative, 1889–90, 1891–95
TYSON, John R.
   b. Lowndes Co., Ala., Nov. 28, 1856
   d. Rochester, Minn., Mar. 27, 1923
   Chief Justice of Alabama, 1906–09
   U. S. Representative, 1921–23
UNDERWOOD, Oscar W.
   b. Louisville, Ky., May 6, 1862
   d. Fairfax Co., Va., Jan. 25, 1929
   U. S. Representative, 1895–96, 1897–1915
   U. S. Senator, 1915–27

WALKER, John W.
  b. Amelia Co., Va., Apr. 12, 1783
  d. Huntsville, Ala., Apr. 23, 1823
  U. S. Senator, 1819-22
WALKER, Percy
  b. Huntsville, Ala., Dec. 1812
  d. Mobile, Ala., Dec. 31, 1880
  U. S. Representative, 1855-57
WARNER, Willard
  b. Granville, Ohio, Sept. 4, 1826
  d. Chattanooga, Tenn., Nov. 23, 1906
  U. S. Senator, 1868-71
WATTS, Thomas Hill
  b. Conecuh, Ala., Jan. 3, 1819
  d. Montgomery, Ala., Sept. 16, 1892
  Governor of Alabama, 1863-65
WHEELER, Joseph
  b. Augusta, Ga., Sept. 10, 1836
  d. Brooklyn, N. Y., Jan. 25, 1906
  U. S. Representative, 1881-82, 1883,
      1885-1900
WHITE, Alexander
  b. Williamson Co., Tenn., Oct. 16, 1816
  d. Dallas, Tex., Dec. 13, 1893
  U. S. Representative, 1851-53, 1873-75
WHITE, Frank S.
  b. Noxabee Co., Miss., Mar. 13, 1847
  d. Birmingham, Ala., Aug. 1, 1922
  U. S. Senator, 1914-15
WILEY, Ariosto A.
  b. Barbour Co., Ala., Nov. 6, 1848
  d. Bath Co., Va., June 17, 1908
  U. S. Representative, 1901-08
WILEY, Oliver C.
  b. Pike Co., Ala., Jan. 30, 1851
  d. Pike Co., Ala., Oct. 18, 1917
  U. S. Representative, 1908-09

WILLIAMS, Jeremiah N.
   b. Barbour Co., Ala., May 29, 1829
   d. Clayton, Ala., May 8, 1915
   U. S. Representative, 1875-79
WILLIAMS, Thomas
   b. Virginia, Aug. 11, 1825
   d. Wetumpka, Ala., Apr. 13, 1903
   U. S. Representative, 1879-85
WINSTON, John Anthony
   b. Madison Co., Ala., Sept. 4, 1812
   d. Mobile, Ala., Dec. 21, 1871
   Governor of Alabama, 1853-57
YANCEY, William L.
   b. Warren Co., Ga., Aug. 10, 1814
   d. Montgomery, Ala., July 28, 1863
   U. S. Representative, 1844-46
   Confederate Senator, 1862-63

OUTLINE OF STATE CONSTITUTION

The complete current text of the State Constitution appears in the Columbia University volumes of Constitutions of the United States, National and State. *The following outline of the text adopted in 1901 and the amendments to date is based on the edited form of the text in these volumes.*

VI. *Judicial Department*

VII. Impeachments

VIII. Suffrage and Elections

IX. Representation

X. Exemptions

XI. Taxation

XIV. Education

XV. Militia

X.   Poll tax exemption amendment (1922)
XI.   Road bond issue amendment (1922)
XII.   Mobile port amendment (1922)
XIII.   Municipal tax amendment (1922)
XIV.   Poll tax exemption amendment (1922)
XV.   Drainage system, public roads, seawall
          (1922)
XVI.   Mobile county school tax (1922)
XVII.   Taxation in certain municipalities (1922)
XVIII.   Mobile county road bonds (1922)
XIX.   Walker county special road tax (1922)
XX.   Tax elections in certain school districts
          in Lawrence county (1922)
XXI.   Art. XXA. State roads, highways and
          bridges – bond issue (1927)
XXII.   Drainage districts (1928)
XXIII.   Repeal of Sec. 219; inheritance and
          estate taxes (1931)
XXIV.   Proposal of amendment and election (1933)
XXV.   Income taxes (1933)
XXVI.   State debts (1933)
XXVIA.   Suspension of restriction on diminishing
          public salaries, etc. (1933)
XXVI.   Amendment of Sec. 229 (1935)
XXVIII.   Costs, fees, salaries, etc., in Mobile
          county (1935)
XXIX.   Mobile county bonds (1935)
XXX.   Lawrence county bonds (1935)
XXXI.   Taxation in municipality of Attalla
          (1935)
XXXII.   Tax elections in certain school districts
          in Lawrence county (1935)
XXXIII.   Regulation of salaries, etc., of certain
          public officers (1935)
XXXIV.   Tax for malaria control in Limestone
          county (1938)
XXXV.   Sheriff succeeding self (1938)
XXXVI.   Erection, etc., of jail in Morgan county
          (1938)

SELECTED DOCUMENTS

The five documents ·selected for this section have been chosen to reflect the interests or attitudes of the contemporary observer or writer. Documents relating specifically to the constitutional development of Alabama will be found in the opening volume of Sources and Documents of United States Constitutions, *a companion reference collection to the Columbia University volumes previously cited.*

A DESCRIPTION OF THE ALABAMA TERRITORY

Anticipating the creation of a separate Alabama Territory in 1817, the War Department undertook to have the boundaries surveyed and, more importantly, to evaluate the resources therein as well as the remnants of the Indian claims after the Creek War. The following report by William Barnett to the Acting Secretary of War suggests the difficulties of making such a study.

Huntsville, M. T. 12th March, 1817.

Sir, After the receipt of your letter of the 8th January, I lost no time in setting out to meet General Coffee at Huntsville, for the purpose of running & marking the lines alluded to. Before my arrival at that place, however, I learnt that the General, disappointed in meeting me, & ignorant of the cause of my absence, already explained to your Department, had exercised the discretion with which, in that case, he was invested; and, having completed the lines alone, had returned to his residence in Tennessee. Thither, therefore, I shaped my course, and had an interview with him. It appeared, in the conference, that so much of the Eastern boundary with the Cherokees, specified in the Treaty with that Tribe, as extends from the junction of the West Fork of Wills' Creek with the main stream to the Ten Islands on the Coosa River, had not been ascertained by actual survey. It was deemed proper, agreeably to the suggestion in your letter of the 8th January to General Coffee, that this should be done. Accordingly, Mr. LeRoy May was selected as Surveyor for that purpose; with whom I set out from Murfreesboro' on the 16th and reached Huntsville on the 19th of the last month. Here, by advice by General Coffee, I employed Mr. Hunter Peal to protract the field-notes of the several surveys, and immediately set him to work in draughting the same into plats, while Mr. May was engaged in running unfinished line. The gentleman returned on the 3rd instant, made his report, and was discharged. My time since has been employed in attending to the completion of the Plats, which were not finished till today. I now send them to General Coffee, for his examination & signature, who will give them, respectively, the destination required by the second section of the Act of the 3 March 1815.

Having been confined, pretty generally, to the lines run under my direction, I have been enabled to make but little examination into the interior of the general Survey now presented. Yet such knowledge as I possess, & such remarks as suggest themselves to my recollection, are very cheerfully submitted.

The Country from the Mouth of Wills' Creek, down the Coosa to Wetumpke, or the Great Falls, is generally poor, broken, & somewhat mountainous; well-watered, and interspersed occasionally with small bodies of rich land, particularly near the mouths of Chokolocko & Kiomulga Creeks, & also in the vicinity of Fort Williams - the reserve, however, excepted: - at or near which places we lose sight of the Blue-limestone.

The land in the Fork of the Coosa & Talapoosa, within the lines, is low & flat, but of good quality; as well as the land on the East of the Talapoosa from its junction with the Coosa to the mouth of Oakfukshea, & up the same to the 10 mile point. This whole district, however, is badly watered, and has every indication of being unhealthy.

From the ten mile point on the Ofukshea to the mouth of Summochechobe, crossing the head waters of Conaca & Yellow-Water, to the streams which empty into the Chatahouche, it is a high well-watered country; having a growth generally of long-leaved pine, interspersed, however, with handsome tracts of Oak & Hiccory land of a soft gray soil: - well calculated for raising Stock, and the better sort suited to the culture of Cotton. This district may, from its appearance, be pronounced to be healthy.

From the Chatahouche to Flint River the country is much more level, but affords less good land; water is scarce, & not good: - and, on the whole, it must be considered to be unhealthy.

From Flint River to the Georgia line, I do not recollect any land whatever fit for cultivation. It is low, flat, excessively poor, & badly watered; abounding in Cyprus ponds, Bay-galls & Saw-Palmetto-flats: - fit only for present occupants, Gofers, Salamanders & Bull-Snakes.

From the mouth of Wills' Creek to Camp Coffee, on the Tennessee, the country is generally mountainous, interspersed with many rich flats and coves - and is well watered & healthy.

From Camp Coffee to the Flat Rock on Bear Creek, or rather to the point at which a direct line from the one to the other would cross the present line from the mouth of Caney Creek to the Cotton-Gin-Port on the Tombeckbe, is about 75 miles, and presents an almost entirely unbroken body of fine fertile land, well supplied, for the most part, with good springs of water. It is sufficiently high, & has all the indications of health. This beautiful & extensive valley is supposed to average twenty miles in breadth, the Mountains verging nearer to the Tennessee River at the before mentioned points. There can be no doubt that this whole district is admirably adapted to the Culture of Cotton. Near the head of Caney Creek is a large body of Iron-Ore which is said to be very rich.

From the Flat-Rock on Bear Creek to Fort Strother on the traverse line formerly run, which is traced on the Plat, is one continued chain of mountains, except 14 or 15 miles of level land, commencing within six miles of Gaines' Road. Proceeding from the Rock, this valley bears to the South. The land seen by me is not rich. From appearances I was inclined to believe that a good Road might very probably be obtained, in this direction, from the Muscle-Shoals to the Falls of the Black-Warrior.

Of the Country North of the Tennessee River, I do not feel myself specially called on to speak: yet, it may, perhaps, be deemed neither impertinent nor improper to state, that every information I can collect, as well as my own observation, justify me in rating it very highly. It is, in general, remarkably level; not quite so well watered, in some parts, as might be wished; occasionally thin; but containing numerous extensive bodies of first rate land, admirably adapted to the Cotton Culture - resembling strongly, in many important features, the County of Madison which bounds it on the East. What is called the Limestone Country is equal, if not superior, to any in any part of the three Cessions. Many other small streams flow thro' delightful lands. Some of the low-grounds of Elk River are very valuable. Shoal Creek abounds in Iron Ore, & affords some of the finest sites for mills & machinary any where recollected.

The Coosa River, so far as I had an opportunity of examining it, does not at present afford a safe & valuable navigation for Boats of any considerable burthen. Many obstacles present themselves, especially from Fort Williams to Wetumpke. The Great Falls, together with the shoal of 10 or 12 miles in extent immediately above, appear to forbid an attempt, except at great expense, to force any thing like an advantageous navigation. Whether there are any considerable impediments below the Falls, or what is the general depth of the stream, I am not informed.

The Cahaba is said to be navigable for Boats to its Falls, distant from Ditto's Landing, just below Chickasaw Island, on the

Tennessee, about 120 miles: and in the neighborhood of the Falls, both above & below, there is said to be a valley of very inviting land, with the finest Springs, & the fairest prospect of health.

Of the Tombeckbe I have nothing new to offer: but the Black-Warrior is by many thought to be superior in its promise of a good navigation. It is, in fact, the longer stream. Boats ascend even now to the Falls, distant from Ditto's Landing about 100 miles, & nearly the same from the Muscle Shoals.

At the Falls of both these Rivers, the Cahaba & Black-Warrior, it is highly probably that respectable towns will spring up at no very distant day: - and there can be little doubt that the neighborhood of the Muscle Shoals is destined to be the site of a great & flourishing City.

There is still another subject, not embraced, indeed, within the letter of your instructions, but so intimately connected with the condition & value of the Ceded Territory, that I trust I may be excused for offering a remark or two upon it.

It must not be forgotten, then, that these lands, tho' unsold, & tho', in great part, not even surveyed, are by no means destitute of inhabitants. On the contrary, some districts are quite populous, & settlements are scattered here & there almost over its whole extent. In the valley North of the Mountains & South of the Tennessee, I suppose there were 300 families who made Corn last year; and, doubtless, at this time the number is considerably increased. On the South Side of the Mountains, including the waters of the Alabama & Tombigby, the settlements last year were more numerous in proportion to the good lands, & in many places much more dense. Where water was scarce, it was not uncommon to see from four to eight families encamped at one Spring: and there is every reason to believe that the population of this district is, likewise, greatly increased. If this state of things be long suffered to continue, it is very much to be feared that such a species of Society will grow out of it as neither to enhance the price of the lands at the Sales, nor the peace, comfort & good order of the future Settlers: - to say nothing of its effects on the intruders themselves. Strife already prevails, in some parts, as to the right of occupancy, & the extent of ground which that right covers: and such disputes have, in some cases, produced blood-shed.

It is, surely, every way desirable that such a state of things should be speedily arrested. Yet, whatever I may think of that policy which permits settlements to be made on unsold lands at all, and of the indulgence which, in this instance, was last year extended by Congress, I feel it my duty to say, that, in my opinion, the time for removing these intruders is past. Such a measure, at this time, would be productive of incalculable distress. Removal would be to many only another name for total ruin. Before the order of removal could be inforced, the means of raising crops in any of the adjacent legal Counties would no longer be offered to their acceptance, since all the disposable cleared land is already rented out for the year. Many of these unhappy people have expended almost the whole of their little all in reaching the forbidden land; and are utterly incapable of returning, if they wished to do so. Besides, now to remove them, is not only to inflict on them the heaviest losses & evils, but would deprive the United States of the most considerable advantage derived from the irregular & unlicensed system of settlement - the provisions & means of support which they prepare & accumulate for the use of those who afterwards settle legally & by purchase: - and in this respect, it must be confessed, that this race of men is not without its value.

It seems to me that the best policy now, in the choice of the Government, the most effectual remedy for the evils alluded to, is to have these lands surveyed & put in market as speedily as possible. Introduce into these Settlements the sway of the laws, & they will soon be purified & regenerated. For this reason, among others, I could heartily wish that a new Surveyor's District might be established over the late acquisitions from the Cherokees & Chickasaws. This I think advisable on many accounts. It is my opinion that if the Northern part of the purchase were brought first into market, it would increase the amount of Sales in the whole Territory. As that part is much the most desirable on account of its superior health, fertility, & capacity to sustain a condensed & numerous population, the monied Capital will probably be held up for those lands: and many will refuse to buy below, in the hope of pleasing themselves better in this quarter, who would buy there when there was no longer a prospect of buying here. Besides, these lands will unquestionably sell high & rapidly; and the sales here might give a tone to those below.

I have the honor to be, Very respectfully, Your obedient Servant,

William Barnett, US Commissioner

George Graham Esquire Acting Secretary of War, Washington City.

COMMISSION OF THE TERRITORIAL GOVERNOR

William Wyatt Bibb, a native of Virginia, had been trained in medicine and engaged in practice in Georgia; served three terms in the U.S. House of Representatives before being selected to fill the Senate seat of William H. Crawford, who served as Secretary of War and Treasury under both Presidents Madison and Monroe. It was through Crawford's influence that Monroe named Bibb as the first governor of the new territory.

September 25, 1817

JAMES MONROE, President of the United States of America,
To all who shall see these presents, Greeting:
Know Ye, That reposing special Trust and Confidence in the Patriotism, Integrity and Abilities of WILLIAM W. BIBB of the State of Georgia, I do appoint him Governor in and over the Alabama Territory, and do authorize and empower him to execute and fulfil the duties of that Office according to law; and to Have and to Hold the said Office with all the powers, privileges and emoluments to the same of right appertaining until the end of the next Session of the Senate of the United States, and no longer, unless the President of United States for the time being should be pleased sooner to revoke and determine this Commission.

In Testimony whereof, I have caused these Letters to be made patent, and the Seat of the United States to be hereunto affixed. Given under my hand at the City of Washington the twenty fifth day of September, A.D. 1817; and of the Independence of the United States of America, the Forty Second.

JAMES MONROE,

By the President,

JOHN QUINCY ADAMS, Secretary of State.

THE ALABAMA RESOLUTIONS OF 1860

The Cincinnati convention of the Democratic Party in 1856 sought to accommodate all sections on the slavery question. While accepting the generalized statements of that convention, the Alabama Democrats insisted upon a more unequivocal pro-salvery platform in the 1860 convention at Charleston, S.C. The resolutions prepared by the state Democratic party for the national convention reflect the constitutional theory upon which the secession movement was soon to be based.

Resolved, by the Democracy of the State of Alabama in Convention assembled, That holding all issues and principles upon which they have heretofore affiliated and acted with the National Democratic party to be inferior in dignity and importance to the great question of slavery, they content themselves with a general reaffirmance of the Cincinnati platform as to such issues, and also indorse said platform as to slavery, together with the following resolutions:

Resolved, That the Constitution of the United States, is a compact between sovereign and co-equal States, united upon the basis of perfect equality of rights and privileges.

Resolved, further, That the Territories of the United States are common property, in which the States have equal rights, and to which the citizens of any State may rightfully emigrate, with their slaves or other property recognized as such in any of the States of the Union, or by the Constitution of the United States.

Resolved, further, That the Congress of the United State has no power to abolish slavery in the Territories, or to prohibit its introduction into any of them.

Resolved, further, That the Territorial Legislatures, created by the legislation of Congress, have no power to abolish slavery, or to prohibit the introduction of the same, or to impair by unfriendly legislation the security and full enjoyment of the same within the Territories; and such constitutional power certainly does not belong to the people of the Territories in any capacity, before, in the exercise of a lawful authority, they form a Constitution preparatory to admission as a State into the Union; and their action in the exercise of such lawful authority certainly cannot operate or take effect before their actual admission as a State into the Union.

Resolved, further, That the principles enunciated by Chief Justice Taney, in his opinion in the Dred Scott case, deny to the Territorial Legislature the power to destroy or impair, by any legislation whatever, the right of property in slaves, and maintain it to be the duty of the Federal Government, in *all* of its departments, to protect the rights of the owner of such property in the Territories; and the principles so declared are hereby asserted to be the rights of the South, and the South should maintain them.

Resolved, further, That we hold all of the foregoing prepositions to contain "cardinal principles" - true in themselves - and just and proper and necessary for the safety of all that is dear to us; and we do hereby instruct our delegates to the Charleston Convention to present them for the calm consideration and approval of that body - from whose justice and patriotism we anticipate their adoption.

Resolved, further, That our delegates to the Charleston Convention are hereby expressly instructed to insist that said Convention shall adopt a platform of principles, recognizing distinctly the rights of the South as asserted in the foregoing resolutions; and if the said National Convention shall refuse to adopt, in substance, the propositions embraced in the preceding resolutions, prior to nominating candidates, our delegates to said Convention are hereby positively instructed to withdraw therefrom.

THE LAST CONFEDERATE SURRENDER

The drama of Lee's surrender to Grant at Appomatox in Virginia, with its dignity of treatment of vanquished by victor, was repeated under lesser renowned circumstances at Citronelle in Alabama, where Lt. General Richard Taylor, C.S.A., commanding one of the last effective Southern armies, capitulated to General Edward R.S. Canby, U.S.A. General Taylor later wrote this reminiscence for a volume entitled, Annals of the War, *a series of articles originally published in 1878 in the Phila. Weekly Times.*

To write an impartial and unprejudiced account of exciting contemporary events has always been a difficult task. More especially is this true of civil strife, which, like all "family jars." evolves a peculiar flavor of bitterness. But slight sketches of minor incidents, by actors and eye-witnesses, may prove of service to the future writer, who undertakes the more ambitious and severe duty of historian. The following *memoir pour servir* has this object.

In the summer of 1864, after the close of the Red river campaign, I was ordered to cross the Mississippi, and report my arrival on the east bank by telegraph to Richmond. All the fortified posts on the river were held by the Federals, and the intermediate portions of the stream closely guarded by gunboats to impede and, as far as possible, prevent passage. This delayed the transmission of the order above-mentioned until August, when I crossed at a point just above the mouth of the Red river. On a dark night, in a small canoe, with horses swimming alongside, I got over without attracting the attention of a gunboat, anchored a short distance below. Woodville, Wilkinson county, Mississippi, was the nearest place in telegraphic communication with Richmond. Here, in reply to a dispatch to Richmond, I was directed to assume command of the Department of Alabama, Missippi, etc., with headquarters at Meridian, Mississippi, and informed that President Davis would, at an early day, meet me at Montgomery, Alabama. The military situation was as follows: Sherman occupied Atlanta, Hood lying some distance to the southwest; Farragut had forced the defenses of Mobile Bay, capturing Fort Morgan, etc., and the Federals held Pensacola, but had made no movements into the interior.

Major General Maury commanded the Confederate forces garrisoning Mobile and adjacent works, with Commodore Farrand, Confederate Navy, in charge of several armed vessels. Small bodies of troops were stationed at different points through the department, and Major General Forrest, with his division of cavalry, was in the Northeast Mississippi. Directing the latter officer to move his command across the Tennessee river, and use every effort to interrupt Sherman's communications south of Nashville, I proceeded to Mobile to inspect the fortifications; thence to Montgomery, to meet President Davis. The interview extended over many hours, and the military situation was freely discussed. Our next meeting was at Fortress Monroe, where, during his confinement, I obtained permission to visit him. The closing scenes of the great drama succeeded each other with startling rapidity. Sherman marched, unopposed, to the sea. Hood was driven from Nashville across the Tennessee, and asked to be relieved. Assigned to this duty I met him near Tupelo, North Mississippi, and witnessed the melancholy spectacle presented by a retreating army. Guns, small-arms and accoutrements lost, men without shoes or blankets, and this in a winter of unusual severity for that latitude. Making every effort to re-equip this force, I suggested to General Lee, then commanding all the armies of the Confederacy, that it should be moved to the Carolinas, to interpose between Sherman's advance and his (Lee's) lines of supply, and, in the last necessity, of retreat. The suggestion was adopted, and this force so moved. General Wilson, with a well-appointed and ably-led command of Federal cavalry, moved rapidly through North Alabama, seized Selma, and, turning east to Montgomery, continued into Georgia.

General Canby, commanding the Union armies in the Southwest, advanced up the eastern shore of Mobile bay and invested Spanish Fort and Blakely, important Confederate works in that quarter. After repulsing an assault, General Maury, in accordance with instructions, withdrew his garrisons, in the night, to Mobile, and then evacuated the city, falling back to Meridian, on the line of the Mobile and Ohio Railway. General Forrest was drawn in to the same point, and the little army, less than eight thousand of all arms, held in readiness to discharge such duties as the waning fortunes of the "cause" and the honor of its arms might demand.

Intelligence of Lee's surrender reached us. Staff officers from Johnston and Sherman came across the country to inform Canby and myself of their "convention." Whereupon an interview was arranged between us to determine a course of action, and a place selected ten miles north of Mobile, near the railway. Accompanied by a staff officer, Colonel William M. Levy (now a member of Congress from Louisiana), and making use of a "hand car." I reached the appointed spot, and found General Canby with a large escort, and many staff and other officers. Among these I recognized some old friends, notably General Canby himself and Admiral James Palmer. All extended cordial greetings. A few moments of private conversation with Canby led to the establishment of a truce, to await further intelligence from the North. Forty-eight hours' notice was to be given by the party desiring to terminate the truce. We then joined the throng of officers, and although every one present felt a deep conviction that the last hour of the sad struggle approached, no allusion was made to it. Subjects awakening memories of the past, when all were sons of a loved, united country, were, as by the natural selection of good breeding, chosen. A bountiful luncheon was soon spread, and I was invited to partake of patis, champagne-frappe, and other "delights," which, to me, had long been as lost arts. As we took our seats at the table, a military band in attendance commenced playing "Hail Columbia." Excusing himself, General Canby walked to the door. The music ceased for a moment, and then the strain of "Dixie" was heard. Old Froissart records no gentler act of "courtesie." Warmly thanking General Canby for his delicate consideration, I asked for "Hail Columbia," and proposed we should unite in the hope that our Columbia would soon be, once more, a happy land. This and other kindred sentiments were duly honored in "frappe," and, after much pleasant intercourse, the party separated.

The succeeding hours were filled with a grave responsibility, which could not be evaded or shared. Circumstances had appointed me to watch the dying agonies of a cause that had fixed the attention of the world. To my camps, as the last refuge in the storm, came many members of the Confederate Congress. These gentlemen were urged to go at once to their respective homes, and, by precept and example, teach the people to submit to the inevitable, obey the laws, and resume the peaceful occupations on which society depends. This advice was followed, and with excellent effect on public tranquility.

General Canby dispatched that his government disavowed the Johnston-Sherman convention, and it would be his duty to resume hostilities. Almost at the same instant came the news of Johnston's surrender. There was no room for hesitancy. Folly and madness combined would not have justified an attempt to prolong a hopeless contest.

General Canby was informed that I desired to meet him for the purpose of negotiating a *surrender* of my forces, and that Commodore Farrand, commanding the armed vessels in the Alabama river, desired to meet Rear Admiral Thatcher for a similar purpose. Citronville, some forty miles north of Mobile, was the appointed place; and there, in the early days of May, 1865, the great war virtually ended.

After this, no hostile gun was fired, and the authority of the United States was supreme in the land. Conditions of surrender were speedily determined, and of a character to soothe the pride of the vanquished - officers to retain side-arms, troops to turn in arms and equipments to their own ordnance officers, so of the quartermaster and commissary stores; the Confederate cotton agent for Alabama and Mississippi to settle his accounts with the Treasury Agent of the United States; muster-rolls to be prepared, etc.; transportation to be provided for the men. All this under my control and supervision. Here a curious incident may be mentioned. At an early period of the war, when Colonel Albert Sidney Johnston retired to the south of the Tennesse River, Isham G. Harris, Governor of Tennessee, accompanied him, taking, at the same time, the coin from the vaults of the State Bank of Tennessee, at Nashville. This coin, in the immediate charge of a bonded officer of the bank, had occasioned much solicitude to the Governor in his many wanderings. He appealed to me to assist in the restoration of the coin to the bank. At my request, General Canby detailed an officer and escort, and the money reached the bank intact.

The condition of the people of Alabama and Mississippi was at this time deplorable. The waste of war had stripped large areas of the necessaries of life. In view of this, I suggested to General Canby that his troops, sent to the interior, should be limited to the number required for the preservation of order, and be stationed at points where supplies were more abundant. That trade would soon be established between soldiers and people - furnishing the latter with currency, of which they were destitute - and friendly relations promoted. These suggestions were adopted, and a day or two thereafter, at Meridian, a note was received from General Canby, inclosing copies of orders to Generals Granger and Steele, commanding army corps, by which it appeared these officers were directed to call on me for, and conform to, advice relative to movements of their troops. Strange, indeed, must such confidence appear to statesmen of the "bloody-shirt" persuasion. In due time, Federal staff-officers reached my camp. The men were paroled and sent home. Public property was turned over and receipted for, and this as orderly and quietly as in time of peace between officers of the same service.

What years of discord, bitterness, injustice and loss would not our country have been spared, had the wounds of war healed "by first intention" under the tender ministrations of the hands that fought the battles? But the task was allotted to ambitious partisans, most of whom had not heard the sound of a gun. As of old, the Lion and the Bear fight openly and sturdily - the stealthy Fox carries off the prize.

THE ALABAMA CONSTITUTIONAL CONVENTION

With the opening of the twentieth century, a number of Southern states were drafting new constitutions to cope with a problem which had become increasingly acute after Reconstruction -- the exploitation of Negro voters by political factions. Although a "Bourbon" objective of "white supremacy" also lay behind the disfranchisement strategy, there was little prospect that national opinion was apt to generate any Congressional opposition. Max Bennett Thrasher, a correspondent for the Outlook *magazine, thus found Alabamians quite candid in their discussion of the objectives of the 1901 constitution.*

Outlook, June 22, 1901

The Alabama Constitutional Convention, which is now in session, is composed of one hundred and fifty-five delegates. It will deal with a variety of questions, but two of these transcend all others in importance - the disfranchisement of the negro and the division of the public-school money between the two races according to the amount of taxes which each pays.

At the request of The Outlook I have interviewed several of the leading and representative members of the Convention, and summarize here briefly their opinions on these questions.

The Hon. John B. Knox, Chairman of the Convention:

"No man can say yet what this Convention will do. What we want to do is, within the limits imposed by the Federal Constitution, to establish white supremacy in the State of Alabama. But if we would have white supremacy, we must establish it by law, not by force or fraud. If you teach your boy that it is right to buy a vote, it is an easy step for him to learn to use money to corrupt officials of any class. If you teach him to steal votes, it is an easy step for him to believe that it is right to steal whatever he may need or greatly desire. There is no higher duty resting upon us as citizens than that which requires us to embody in the fundamental law such provisions as will protect the sanctity of the ballot in every portion of the State. Whether or not Alabama will approve the form of relief adopted by other Southern States is not yet known. The delegates to this Convention are pledged not to deprive any white man of the right to vote, but, unless the Convention chooses, this does not extend beyond the life of voters now living. It is a question whether we would be warranted in a course which would tend to condemn any part of our population to a condition of perpetual illiteracy. The States of Mississippi, South Carolina, and Louisiana have rightfully considered that the betterment of the facilities for securing an education of all the people was an essential part of any just and wise scheme for the regulation of the right of suffrage. As Dr. Curry forcibly puts it, 'It will not do to say that you are too poor to educate the people. You are too poor not to educate them.''

Ex-Governor Thomas G. Jones, of Montgomery, Governor of Alabama from 1890 to 1894:

"We are surrounded by many difficulties, one of which was the pledge, made by the Convention which nominated the great majority of the delegates, that we would reform the suffrage in obedience to the Constitution of the United States and yet not disfranchise any white man except for crime. This reduced us to that statesmanship which is said to be 'the science of circumstances.' It stripped us of all power to do many desirable things. The plan offered by me is on the only practical line which will obey the Constitution of the United States and yet not disfranchise any white man. In brief, after the usual exclusions for crime, and want of capacity, and provision for residence, the suffrage was conferred upon those male citizens who paid taxes in each year on property owned by them to the extent of five dollars, or, if the voter owned no property, if he made a contribution to the State of four dollars per annum to the common-school fund, upon soldiers who had served in the wars of the United States, or in the service of the State or the Confederate States, and upon those citizens who, after the Constitution went into effect, to a limited number in each county, were recommended by the grand jury for suffrage by name, and voted for admission to the electorate, by a majority of the voters participating in the election.

"As regards the division of the school fund according to the taxes paid by each race, I strongly protested against it in my inaugural address in 1890, both because of its unconstitutionality and its injustice and inexpediency. I have a resolution condemning such division, which has been referred to the Committee on the Judicial Department. I do not wish to keep the negro in ignorance. I think we owe the duty no less to ourselves that to him to make every effort to give him a common-school education.

"As regards the suffrage qualifications, the opinions of delegates are not sufficiently developed to enable me to judge. I believe that the outcome will be a poll-tax or property qualification, but there are quite a number who wish to try something after the way of the Mississippi plan, and some who wish to put in the grandfather clause. For many reasons, I do not favor any such provisions.

"I do not think the Convention will divide the school fund according to race. The educational qualification will not be adopted, because it would disfranchise a good many whites as well as negroes, and because of the abuses and corruption growing out of the determination of the possession of such qualities when left to a board of registrars.

"There will be considerable debate, but the great majority of the members of the Convention are ready to be informed by discussion, and will probably come to a decision as soon as is consistent with orderly parliamentary proceedings and prudence. I do not believe one delegate in twenty came to the Convention with any preconceived opinion. Every one is studying the question, and there are few not open to argument."

General William C. Oates, member of Congress 1881-1895, and Governor of Alabama in 1895-6:

"I am in favor of letting every one of intelligence - not necessarily book-learning - and good character vote. I would have a Board of Registrars, consisting of three intelligent and discreet men, as non-partisan as possible - not more than two to belong to the same party. These men should be appointed by the Governor with the consent of the Senate. The suffrage should be allowed to all persons except those convicted of crime punishable by imprisonment in the penitentiary, idiots or insane, or persons of notoriously bad character - tramps, paupers, or a man who has sold his vote or bought the vote of another, or who has been convicted of other fraud or bribery to procure his own election or that of another person; provided these persons have paid a poll tax.

"I am opposed to any change in the plan of dividing the school money, as a lawyer and as a man. We recognize that the negroes are of an inferior race to the white man, but they are among us. They are the best laborers we shall ever have. We have extended a helping hand to them. I am opposed to drawing it back. While this must be a white man's government, the responsibility is all the stronger upon the white man to see that the negro is treated rightly. When a man of that race has established a good character, I want him to participate in the election. I am a large taxpayer, and I don't regret the part of my tax which goes to help educate the negro. Ours is largely an agricultural State, and it is not the duty of the people of the State, nor to its interest, to educate the children of either race beyond the primary schools, which by the laws of this State embrace all the branches necessary for a fair English education. I do not think it right nor wise to tax property-owners beyond that point, but up to that point it is the duty of both races, and for the best. If higher education is desired, the individuals should pay for it.

"I think that these views are those of a majority of the delegates, and that they will be adopted. The ablest and most thoughtful delegates to the Convention can be depended upon to move prudently and cautiously. I believe a large majority will readily accede to what they come to believe is best, rather than adhere to any fixed opinions which they may have had when they came to the Convention. I think a considerable number of changes of opinion in the direction of conservatism - favorable to the negro - have already been brought about among the delegates as a result of interchange of views."

The Hon. Cecil Browne, of Talladega, a lawyer who has had considerable legislative experience:

"I favor such a suffrage measure as will make an educational qualfication necessary in order to exercise the franchise, and would except from its operation all who have served as soldiers or sailors in any war of the United States or the Confederacy, and all of their descendants over a certain age; I should prefer fifteen years. Under such a provision, after a few years, the qualification would bear equally upon both races. The immediate effect of this would be to disfranchise more negroes than whites. Then it would become a race between white and black for education. There is now expended in Alabama each year $1,200,000, which our present Constitution provides shall be for the equal education of whites and blacks. I think the white race susceptible of higher education than the colored, and because they pay the bulk of the taxes, I therefore favor some provision by which some voluntary county or municipal tax can be levied and collected from the property of the whites as supplementary to the State funds appropriated for the schools. This, in my opinion, would insure the equal appropriation of the State fund between the children of the two races without regard to color, which is not now the practice. Whether it can be done constitutionally is the question.

"I think the delegates have fixed opinions, but they are too able a body of men not to be susceptible to reason. The sentiment of the Convention is changing in the direction of conservatism. As a general thing, the members came here prepared to disfranchise the negro and take the school money away from him. The general sentiment toward the negro is already more favorable."

The Hon. John T. Ashcraft, a lawyer of Florence and a cotton manufacturer, a teacher for ten years, and a man thoroughly familiar with the educational work in his county:

"I would favor the North Carolina plan for regulating the suffrage. It is clear-cut, offers no inducement to fraud, and all seeming inequalities are to disappear within a reasonable time. The Legislature should be required to establish, organize, and maintain a liberal system of public schools throughout the State for the *equal* benefit of all children for a period of not less than four or five months, and for such longer time as the condition of the treasury and the resources of the State will admit. In addition to this, white districts should be allowed to levy special assessments, and colored districts should be allowed the same right. To divide the school money in proportion to the taxes paid would be to relegate the negro to everlasting heathenism. It would be a travesty upon the efforts of every foreign missionary society in the Southland. I do not think the delegates are pledged to fixed positions. The large majority of them will patiently hear plans and discussions, and then patriotically decide upon some wise course. They are resolved, however, to limit the franchise, as far as possible, to those who by character and tradition are most capable of exercising that sacred right for the highest welfare of the whole State. They are further resolved that the two races shall not longer be bound together hand and foot by unnatural and artificial ties which prevent all growth of race pride in the negro and all exercise of race individuality in the white man. I think the opinion of the Convention is growing more conservative, in favor of the negro."

Senator John T. Morgan, although not a member of the Convention, has prepared and had presented a lengthy proposition on the suffrage question which contains this radical proposition: "Persons who are not citizens of the United States, or who are not descended from a father and mother of the white race, shall not be eligible to any office under the Constitution and laws of Alabama."

General J. B. Graham, of Talladega, Chairman of the Committee on Education, says in a letter published since the Convention assembled:

"To deprive the negro of the right to vote or hold office, and then give him no money for his schools, is to put him in a well and cover him up."

Abernethy, Thomas P. *The Formative Period in Alabama, 1815-1828.* Montgomery, 1922.

Bond, Horace M. *Negro Education in Alabama, a Study in Cotton and Steel.* Washington, 1939.

Brantley, William H. *Three Capitals: A Book About the First Three Capitals of Alabama.* Boston, 1947.

Clark, John B. *Populism in Alabama.* Auburn, 1927.

Denman, Clarence P. *The Secession Movement in Alabama.* Montgomery, 1933.

Dorman, Lewy. *Party Politics in Alabama from 1850-1860.* University, 1949.

Doster, James F. *Alabama's First Railroad Commission, 1881-1885.* University, 1949.

Farmer, Hallie. *The Legislative Process in Alabama: Local and Private Legislation.* University, 1944.

Fleming, Walter L. *Civil War and Reconstruction in Alabama.* Chicago, 1906.

Going, Allen J. *Bourbon Democracy of Alabama, 1874-1890.* University, 1951.

Jack, Theodore H. *Sectionalism and Party Politics in Alabama, 1819-1842.* Menasha, 1915.

Martin, Roscoe C. *The Growth of State Administration in Alabama.* University, 1942.

McMillan, Theodore C. *Constitutional Development in Alabama, 1798-1901.* Chapel Hill, 1955.

Moore, Albert B. *History of Alabama and her People.* Chicago, 1937.

Owen, Marie B. *Story of Alabama.* New York, 1949.

Rogers, William W. *The One-Gallused Rebellion.* Baton Rouge, 1970.

Sellers, James B. *Slavery in Alabama.* University, 1950.

Smith, Charles W. and William V. Holloway. *Government and Politics in Alabama.* University, 1941.

NAME INDEX

NAME INDEX